BOOK ONE

# HAL LEONARD ACOUSTIC GUITAR TAB METHOD

Written by … Schroedl

Contributing Editors: … and Jim Schustedt

ISBN 978-1-4803-6729-6

To access audio, visit:
**www.halleonard.com/mylibrary**

Enter Code
2277-8131-8447-7675

Visit Hal Leonard Online at
**www.halleonard.com**

World headquarters, contact:
**Hal Leonard**
7777 West Bluemound Road
Milwaukee, WI 53213
Email: info@halleonard.com

In Europe, contact:
**Hal Leonard Europe Limited**
1 Red Place
London, W1K 6PL
Email: info@halleonardeurope.com

In Australia, contact:
**Hal Leonard Australia Pty. Ltd.**
4 Lentara Court
Cheltenham, Victoria, 3192 Australia
Email: info@halleonard.com.au

# GETTING STARTED

## PARTS OF THE GUITAR

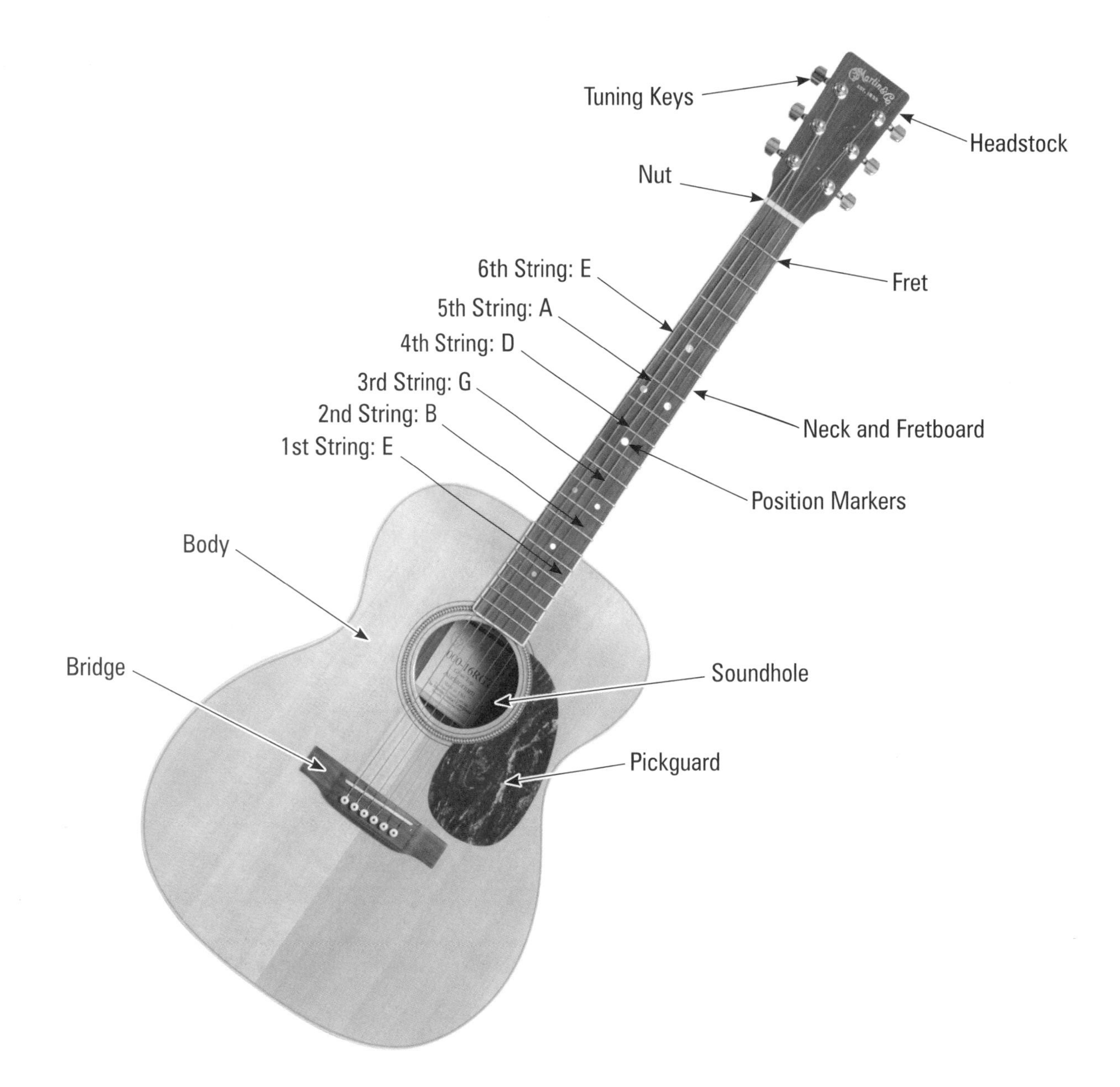


## TUNING

The quickest and most accurate way to get in tune is to use an electronic tuner.

The guitar's six open strings should be tuned to these pitches:

**E (thickest)–A–D–G–B–E (thinnest)**

If you twist a string's tuning key clockwise, the pitch will become lower; if you twist the tuning key counterclockwise, the pitch will become higher.

Adjust the tuning keys until the electronic tuner's meter indicates that the pitch is correct. Or, listen to each string's correct pitch on the Tuning track and slowly turn the tuning key until the sound of the string matches the sound on the track.

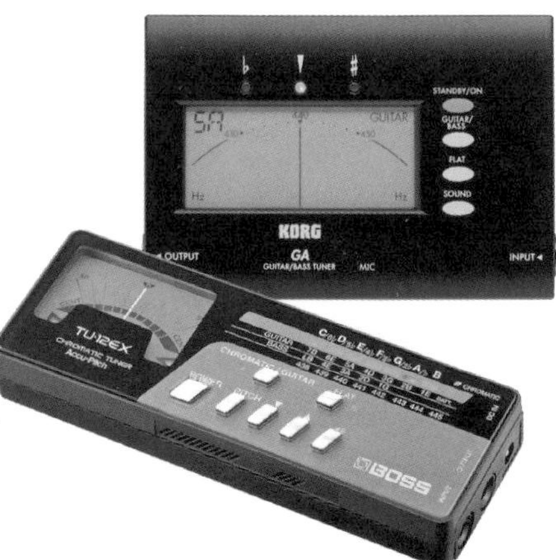

## HOLDING THE GUITAR

Use the pictures below to help find a comfortable playing position. Whether you decide to sit or stand, it's important to remain relaxed and tension-free.

## LEFT-HAND POSITION

Fingers are numbered 1 through 4. Arch your fingers and press the strings down firmly between the frets with your fingertips only.

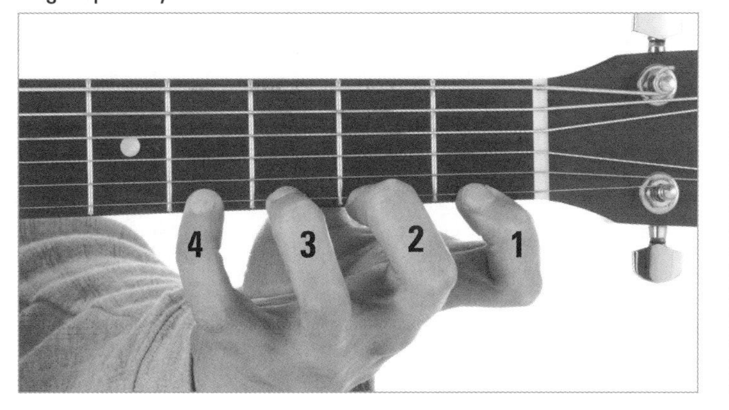


Place your thumb on the underside of the guitar neck. Avoid letting the palm of your hand touch the neck of the guitar.

## RIGHT-HAND POSITION

Hold the pick between your thumb and index finger.

Strike the strings with a downward motion approximately halfway between the bridge and neck, near the bottom of the soundhole.

# YOUR FIRST NOTES

Guitar music is written in a form of notation called **tablature**, or **tab**, for short. Each line represents a fret. The thickest string played open, or not pressed, is the low E note. In tab, an open string is represented with a zero (0). The note F is located on the 1st fret. Press, or "fret," the string with your 1st finger, directly behind the first metal fret.

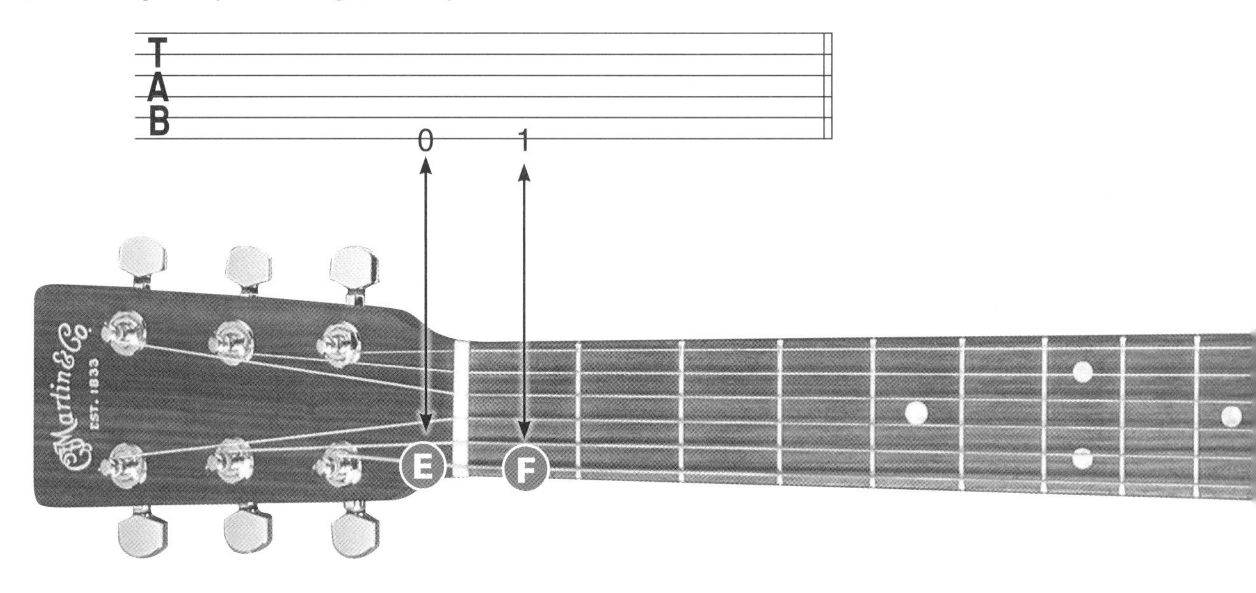


Play the theme from *Jaws* using the notes E and F. Attack the string with a downstroke of your pick. Speed up as the numbers get closer together.

## THEME FROM "JAWS"

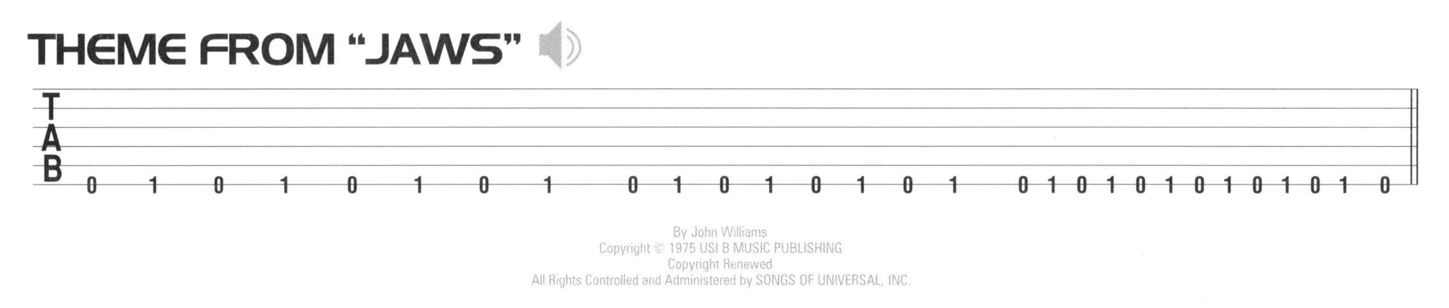



Now try some notes on other strings. Keep the fretted notes held down and let the open strings ring. You'll need to arch your fretting fingers so that they touch *only* the strings with fretted notes.

## UNPLUGGED

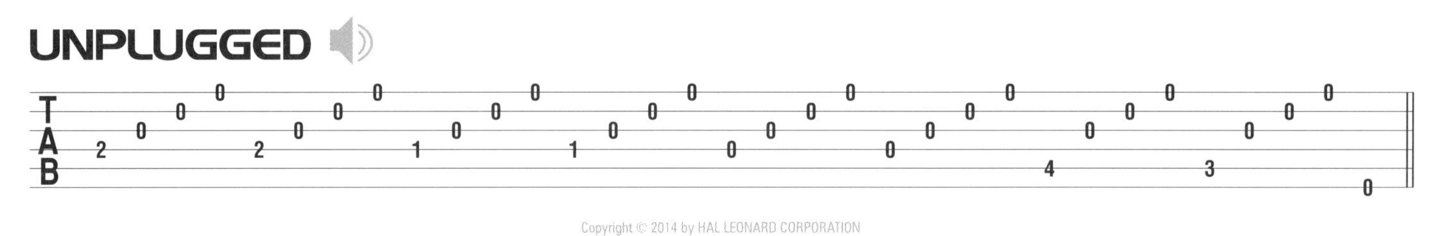



## BATMAN THEME

When tab numbers are stacked, play them together.

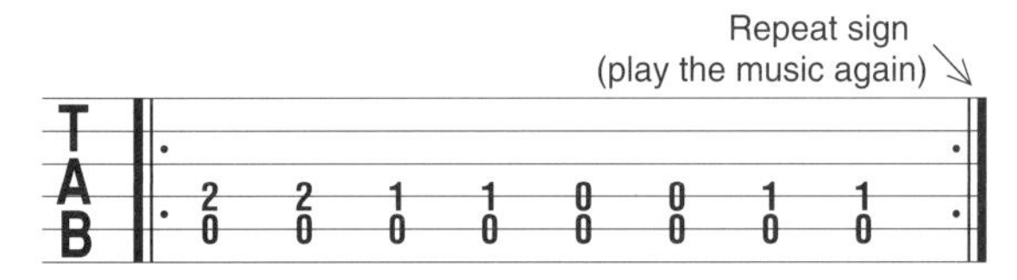




## FREE FALLIN'

Press down two notes at a time to play this hit song by Tom Petty.

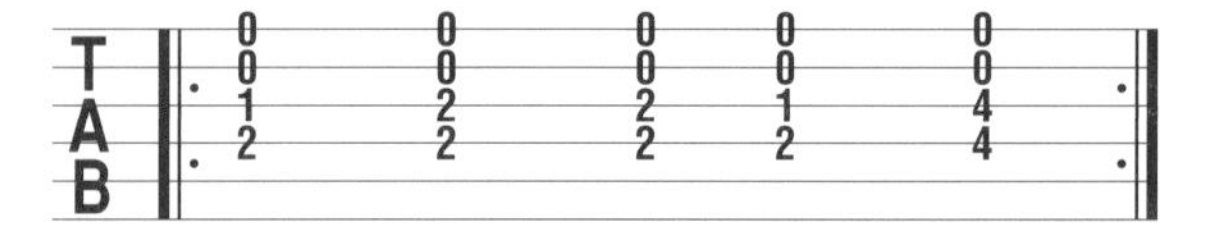

# PLAYING CHORDS

**Chords** are groups of notes played together, usually on four, five, or all six strings. In tab, chords are shown as stacked numbers. Your first chord is E minor, which involves two fretted notes, held down by your 1st and 2nd fingers on the 5th and 4th strings, respectively, while the remaining open strings are allowed to ring. Chords with open strings are called **open chords**.

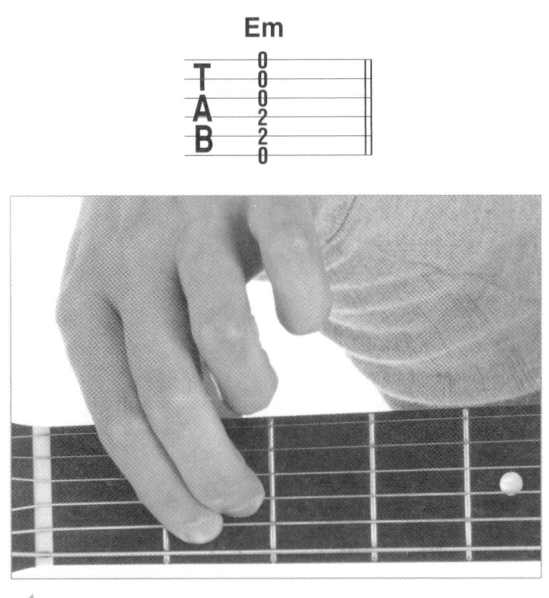


## GET UP STAND UP

When you play all the notes in a chord with a single pick stroke, it's called **strumming**. Strum the E minor chord in a downward motion to play a basic version of this Bob Marley song.

1. Get up, stand up. Stand up for your right.
2. Get up, stand up. Don't give up the fight.

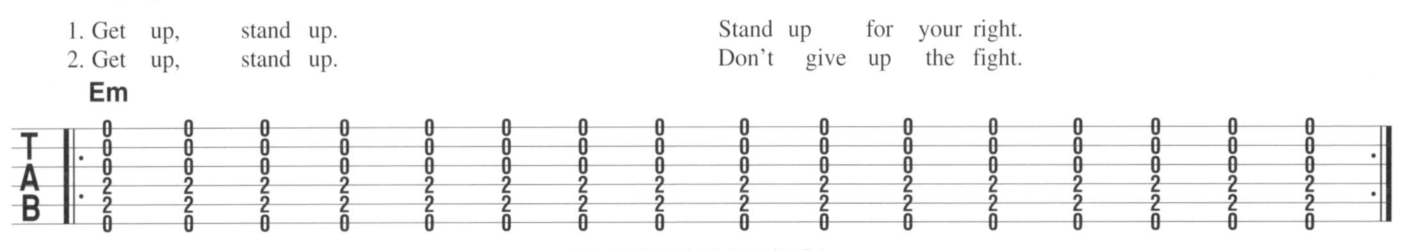




## RAWHIDE

For this classic tune made popular again by the Blues Brothers, alternate playing the open low E string and the E minor chord. The **bar lines** divide up the music to make it easier to read. You'll learn more about this on page 13.

Rollin', rollin', rollin'. Rollin', rollin', rollin'. Rollin', rollin', rollin'. Rawhide!

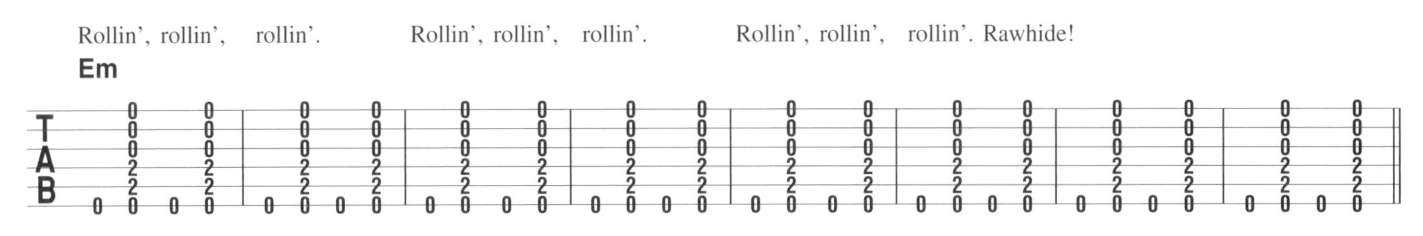




## A HORSE WITH NO NAME

America used an E minor chord as the basis for this hit. For now, don't worry about the name of that other chord; just press the 3rd string down and arch your finger to avoid touching the other strings.

I've been through the desert on a horse with no name. It felt good to be out of the rain.

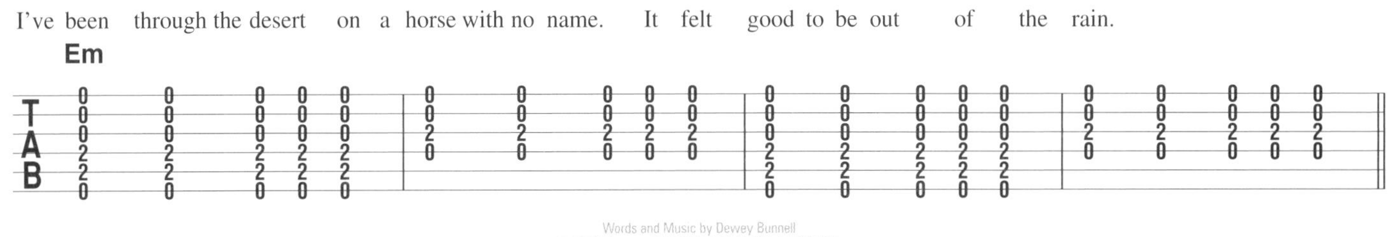

Your next chord is C major. For this chord, you do not play the low E string.

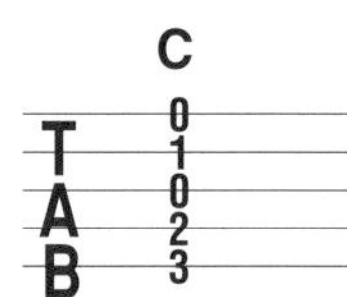


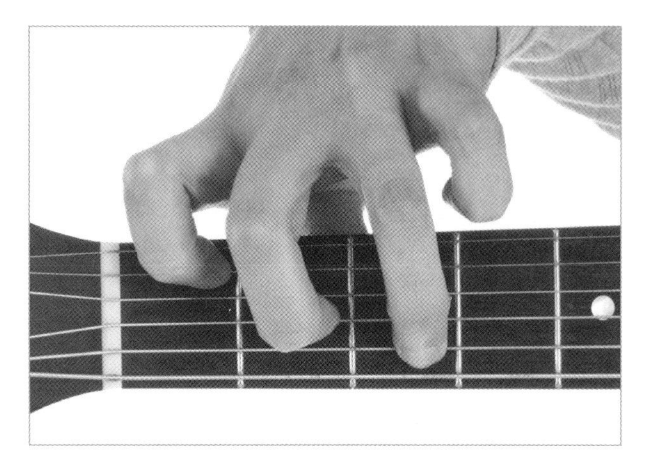

## C TO IT

Strum the C chord using downstrokes. Don't hit the low E string.

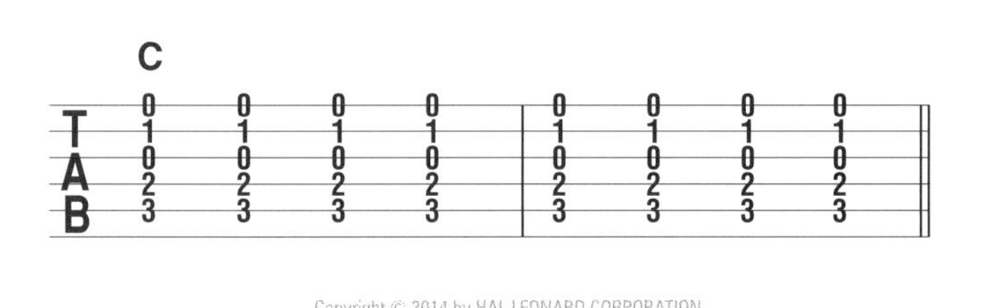




## SPACE ODDITY

When changing from C to Em in this David Bowie song, keep your middle finger on the 4th string.

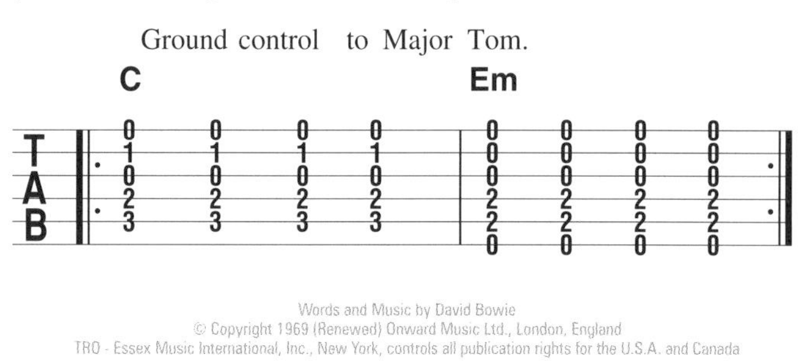




## CHANGING CHORDS

If you had trouble making the change from C to Em in "Space Oddity," try this exercise. Each strum represents one **beat** (or "pulse" of music).

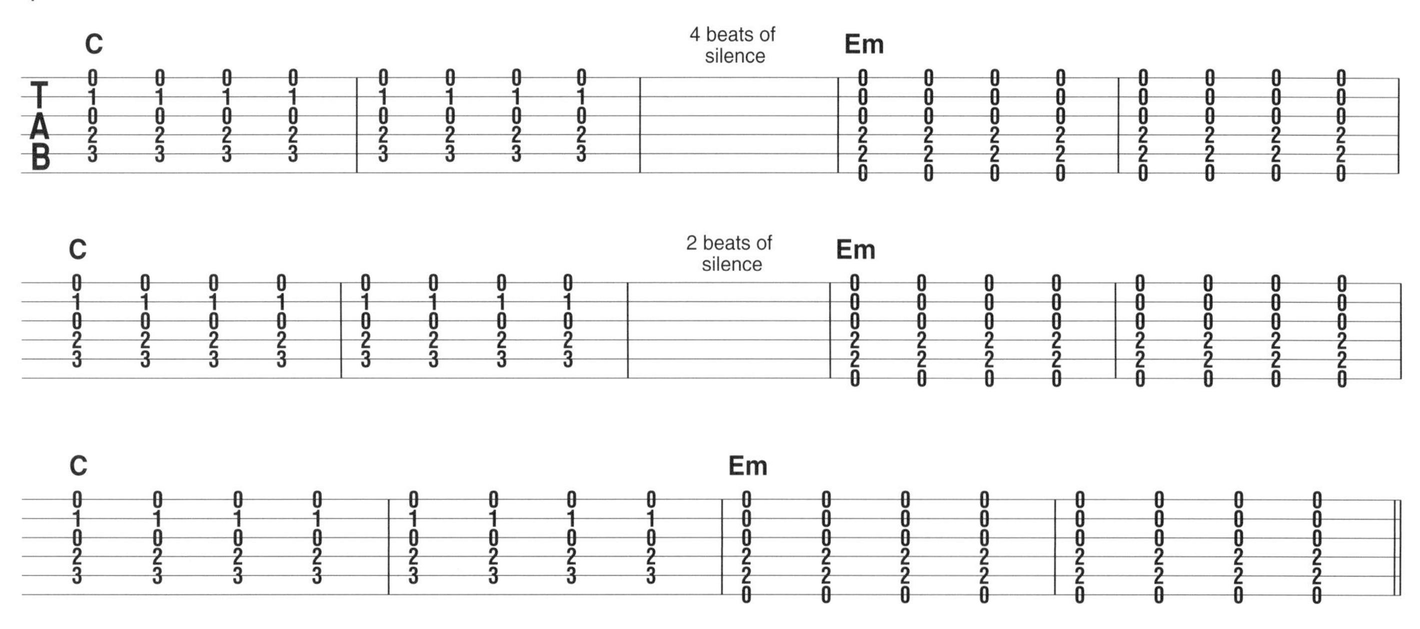

# NEED YOU NOW

For this Lady Antebellum hit, try playing an upstroke after each downstroke, creating an alternating down-up strumming motion.

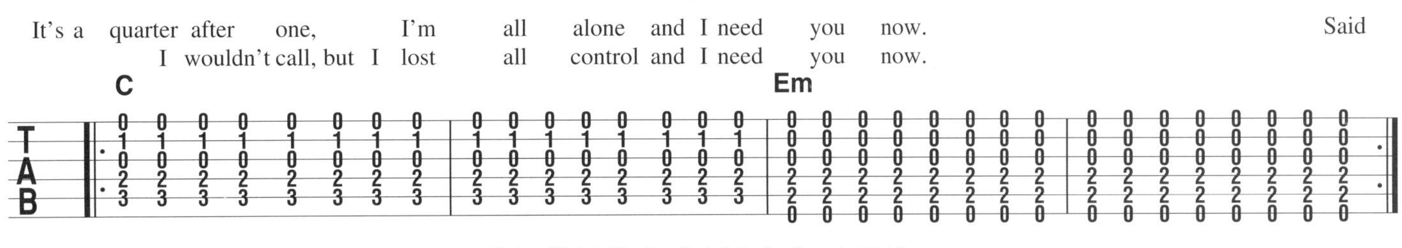




# ELEANOR RIGBY

The Beatles crafted this classic using only two chords for the entire song: C and Em. Use your palm to stop the strings from ringing immediately after each strum. This is called **staccato** and is typically represented with a dot underneath the note or chord.

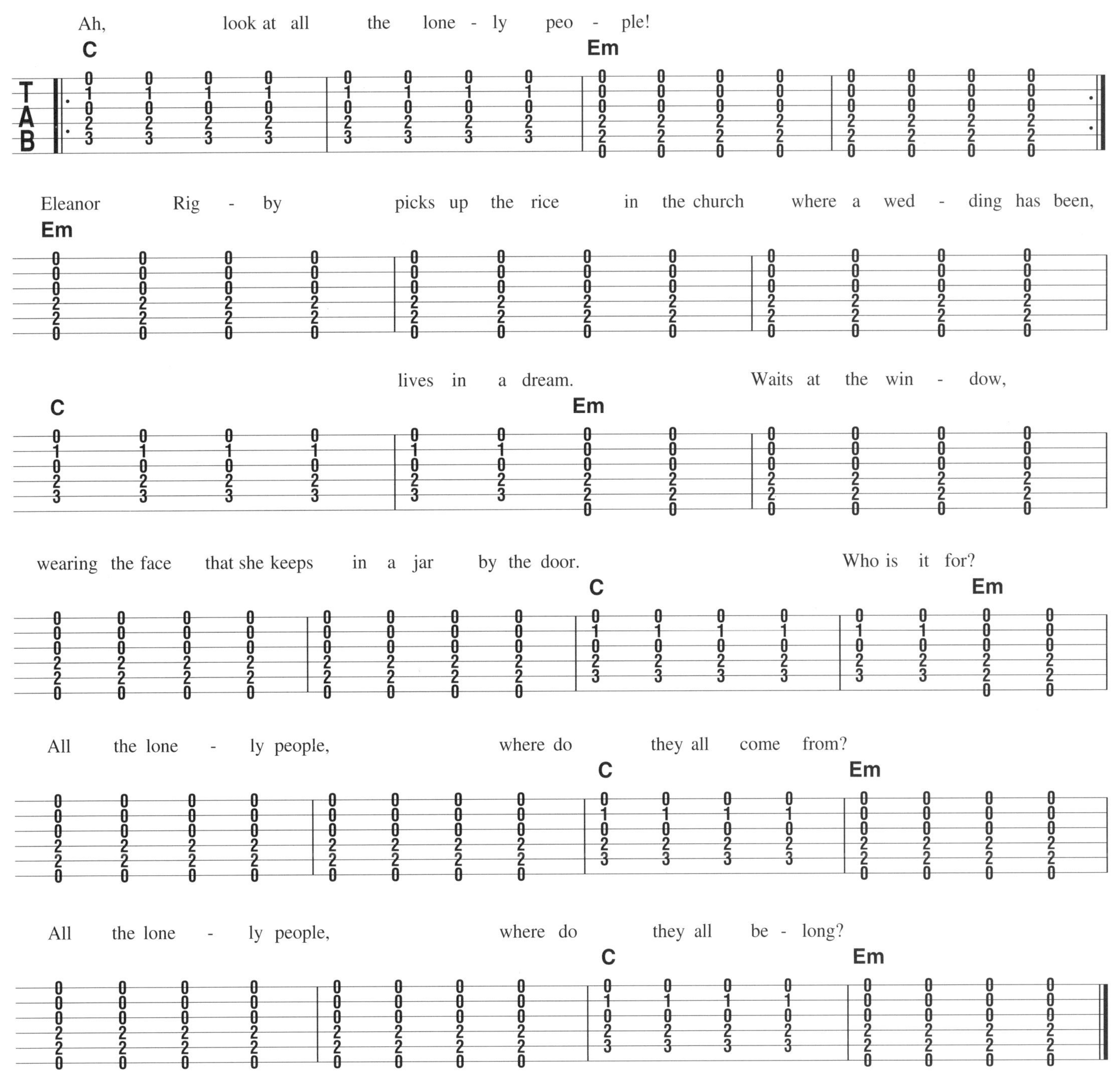

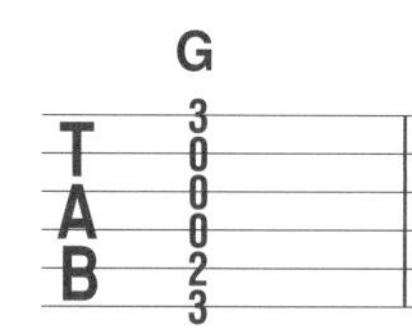


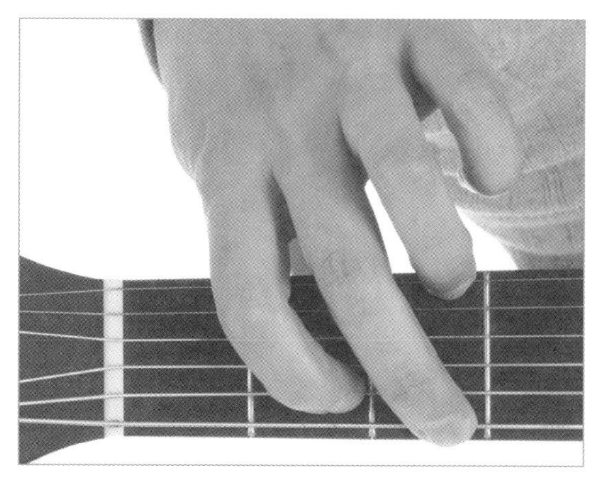

## YELLOW SUBMARINE

Try to keep a steady strum as you change chords for this all-time Beatles favorite.

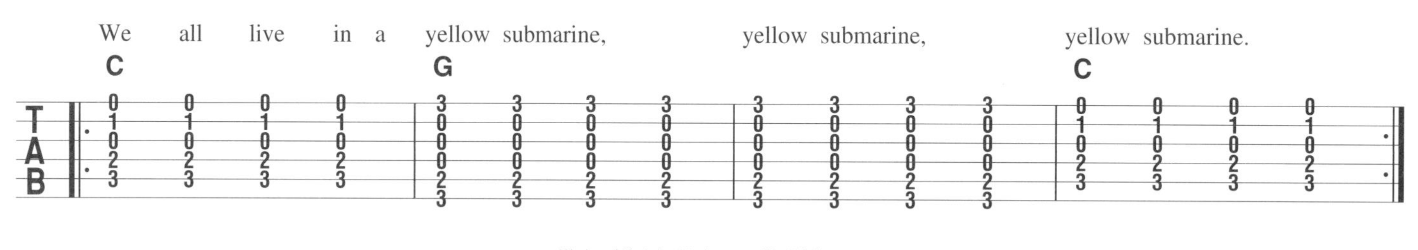




## I GOTTA FEELING

In this monster hit by the Black Eyed Peas, you'll use all three chords you've learned so far. Use steady downstrokes.

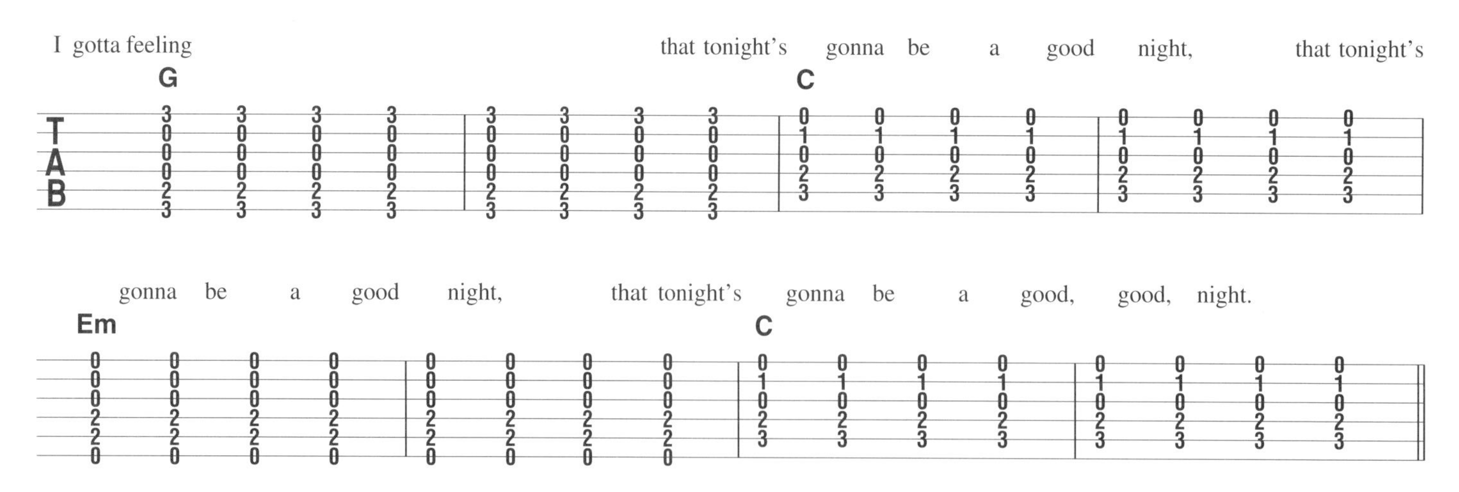

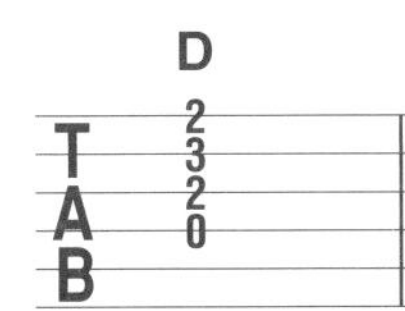


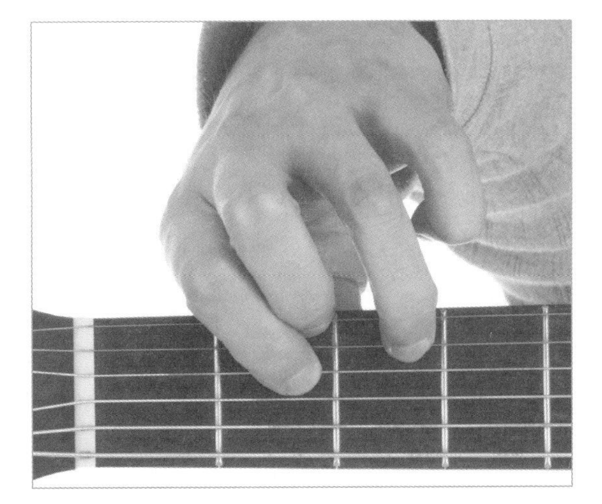

## LAND OF A THOUSAND DANCES

Practice the D chord with this Wilson Pickett classic. Arch your fingers and play on the tips to avoid touching the other strings.

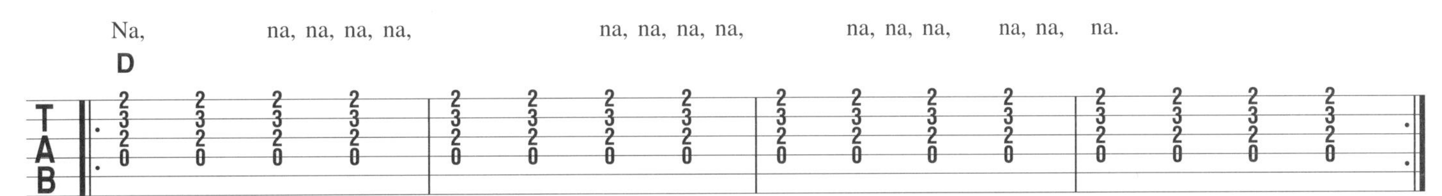




## SCARBOROUGH FAIR

This traditional folk song made popular by Simon & Garfunkel requires you to switch between Em and D chords.

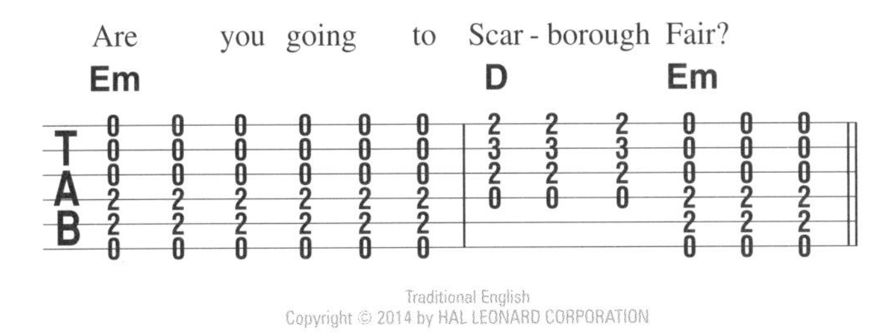




## HEART OF GOLD

Neil Young's intro to this hit also uses Em and D chords.

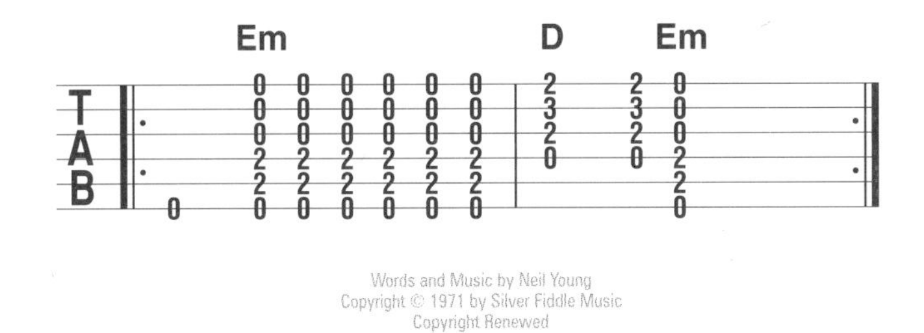




## RING OF FIRE

The chorus of this Johnny Cash song uses G, C, and D chords.

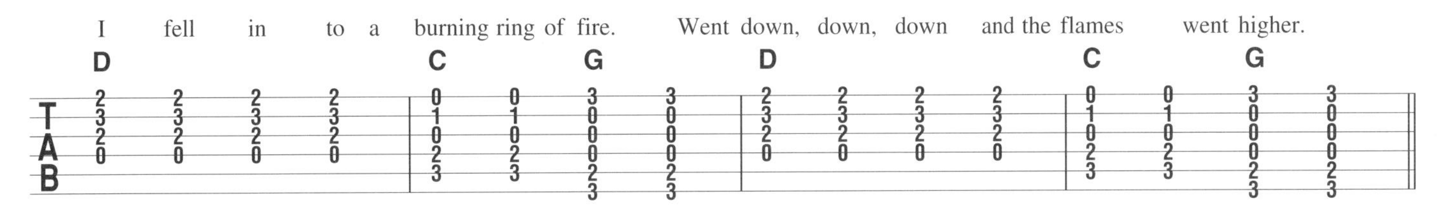

## PROUD MARY

Guitarists often prefer to read from simple **chord charts** rather than follow each strum in tab. Try this approach with this classic by Creedence Clearwater Revival. Feel free to vary your strumming at will, or listen to the accompanying track for guidance.

G

||: 1. Left a good job in the cit - | y, | workin' for the Man every | night and day, |
2. Cleaned a lot of plates in Mem - | phis, | pumped a lot of 'pane down in | New Orleans, |

and I never lost one min - | ute of sleepin', | worryin' 'bout the way things | might have been. |
but I never saw the good | side of the city, un - | til I hitched a ride on a | riverboat queen. |

D | Em

Big wheel keep on turn - | in'. | Proud Mary keep on burn - | in'. Roll - |

G

in', roll - | in', roll - | in' on the riv - er. | :||

G

3. If you come down to the riv | - er | bet you gonna find some peo - | ple who live. |

You don't have to worry 'cause | you have no money; | people on the river are hap - | py to give. |

D | Em

Big wheel keep on turn - | in'. | Proud Mary keep on burn - | in'. Roll - ||

G

||: in', roll - | in', roll - | in' on the riv - er. | Roll - :||



## TAKE ME HOME, COUNTRY ROADS

Now try playing this timeless John Denver hit using a chord chart.

G | Em | D | C G

||: 1. Almost heaven, | West Virginia, | Blue Ridge Mountains, | Shenandoah River. |
2. All my memories | gather 'round her | miner's lady, | stranger to blue water. |

Em | D | C G

Life is old there, | older than the trees, | younger than the mountains, | growing like a breeze. Country |
Dark and dusty, | painted on the sky. | Misty taste of moonshine, | teardrop in my eye. |

D | Em | C

roads, take me | home, to the | place I be - | long: West Vir - |

G | D | C | G

ginia, mountain | momma, take me | home, country | roads. :||

# WILD NIGHT

Van Morrison's "Wild Night" is a certified rock classic and has been covered by numerous artists. It uses all four chords introduced so far and is shown here in chord chart format.

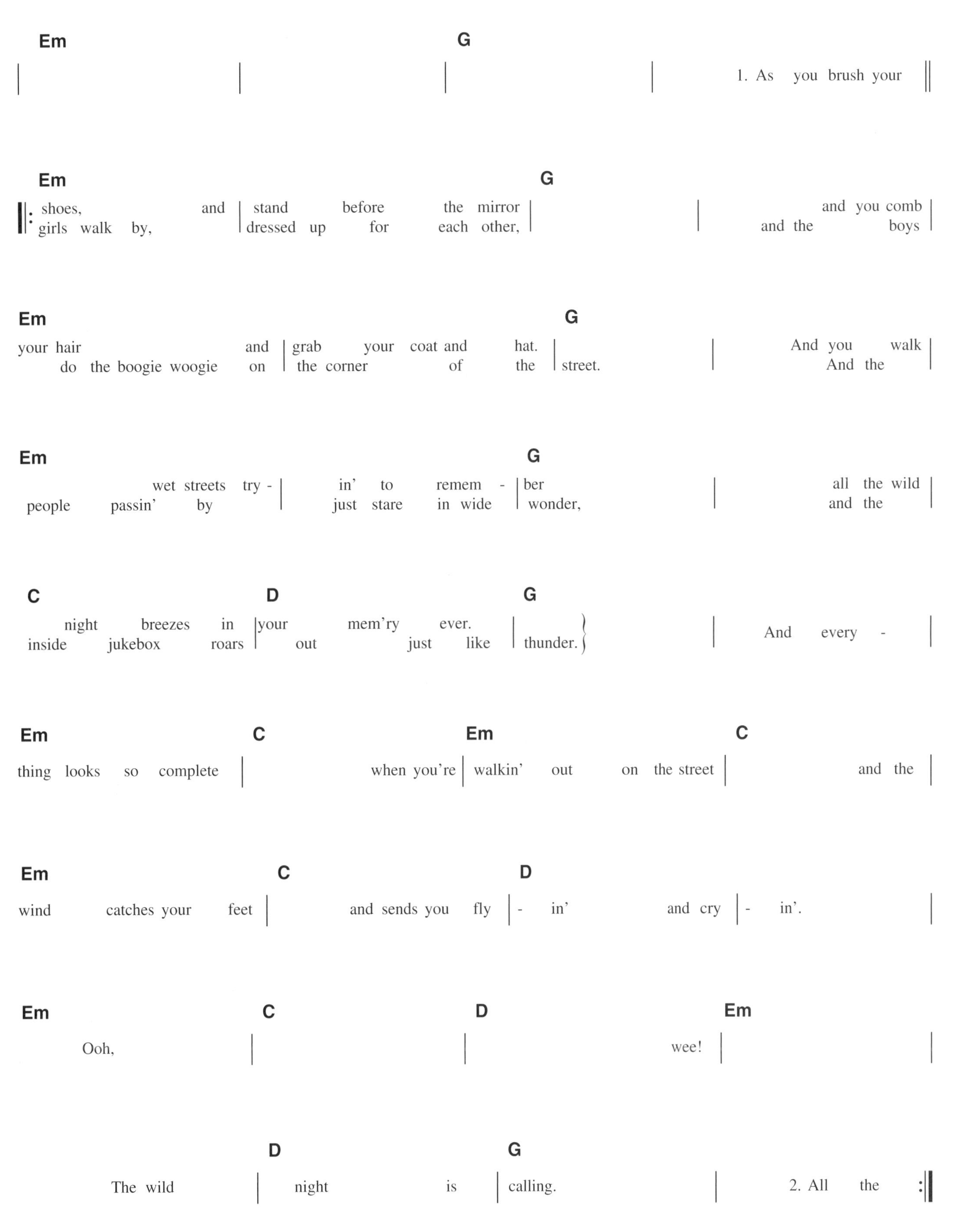

# THE LOW E STRING

Now it's time to learn the notes on your guitar, beginning with the low E string.

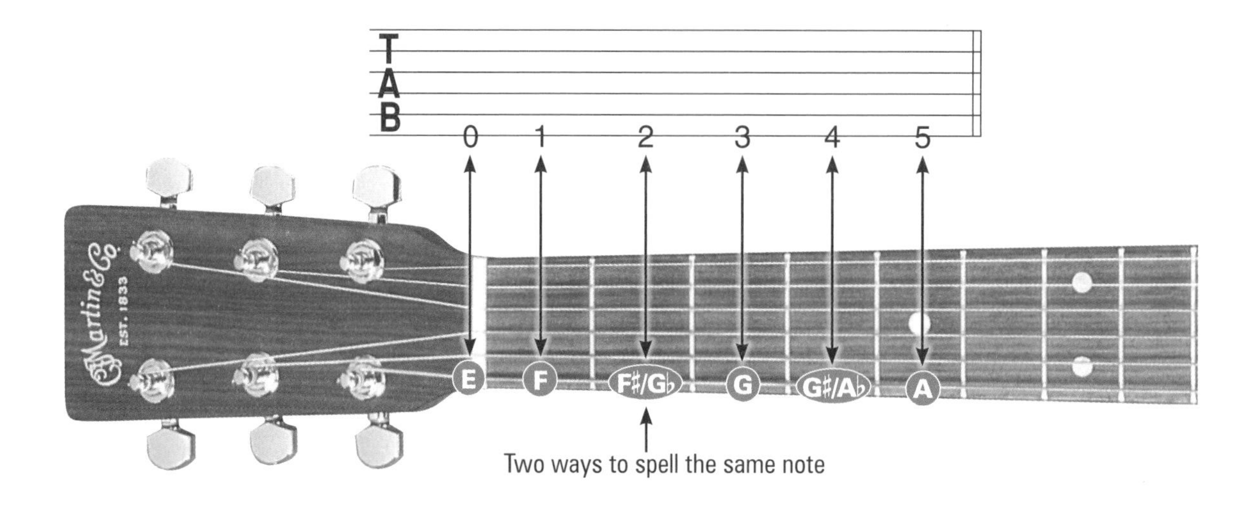


## ACOUSTICA

This exercise for playing notes on the low E string should be played at a steady speed, or **tempo**.

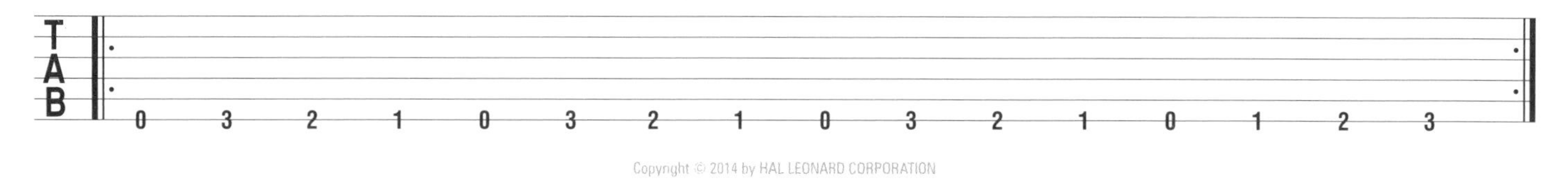




## GREEN ONIONS

This classic jam from Booker T. & the MG's uses the notes E, G, and A.

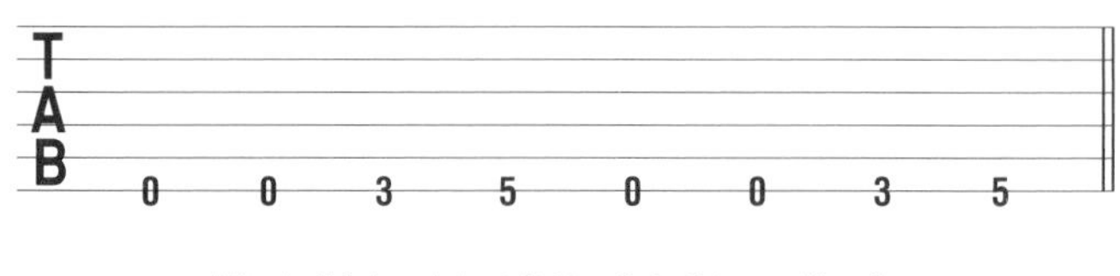




## PETER GUNN

A **riff** is a short, composed phrase that is repeated. The popular riff from "Peter Gunn" is played with notes on the low E string.

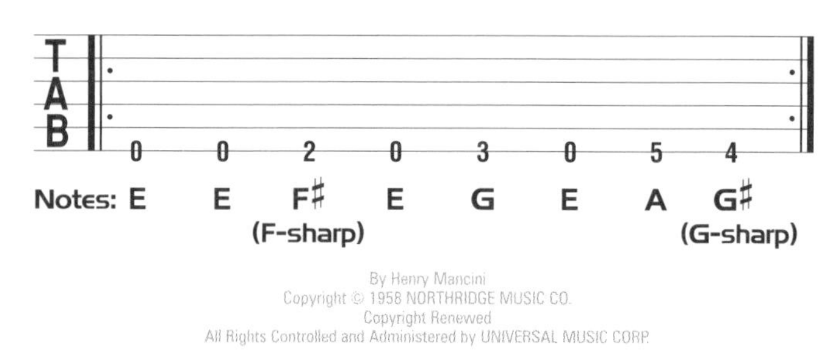




## ALTERNATE PICKING

It's natural for beginning guitarists to use all downstrokes when learning to play single notes, but there's a better and more efficient technique. **Alternate picking** uses alternating downstrokes (⊓) and upstrokes (V) to play single-note lines, similarly to strumming chords in a down-and-up motion. Practice the example below, then go back and play "Green Onions" and "Peter Gunn" using alternate picking.

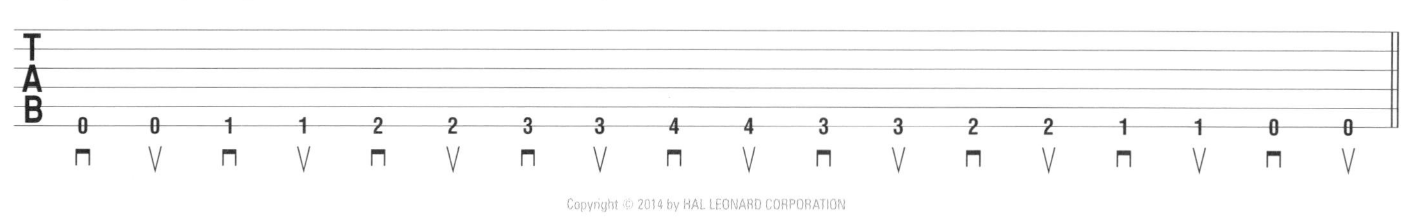

# THE A STRING

Here are the notes within the first five frets of the 5th string, called the A string.

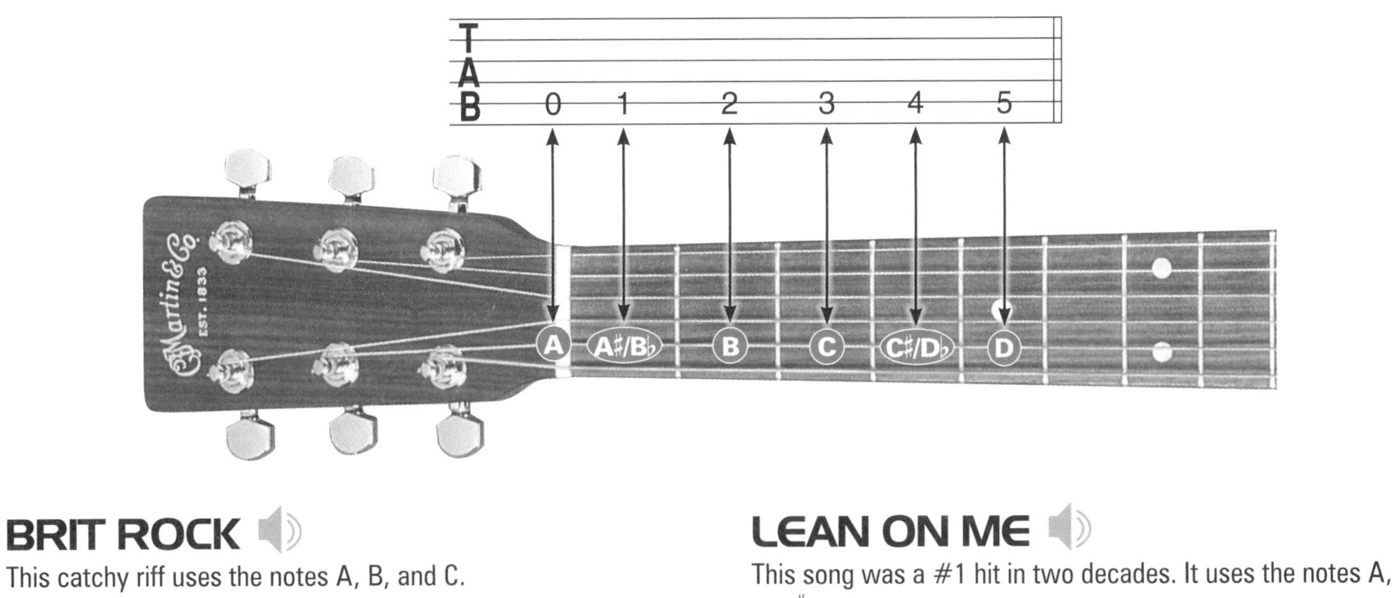


## BRIT ROCK

This catchy riff uses the notes A, B, and C.

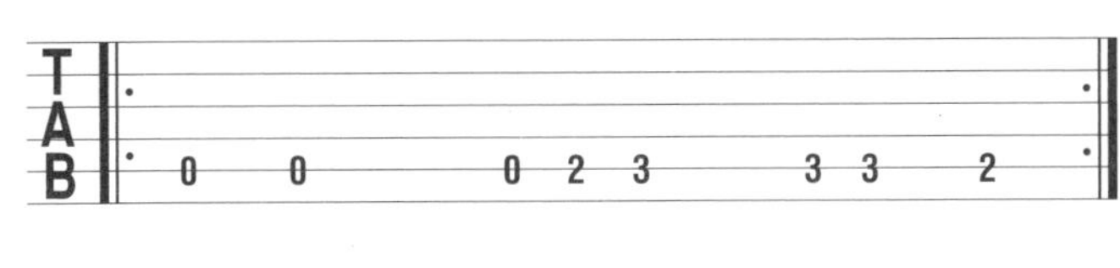




## LEAN ON ME

This song was a #1 hit in two decades. It uses the notes A, B, C♯, and D.

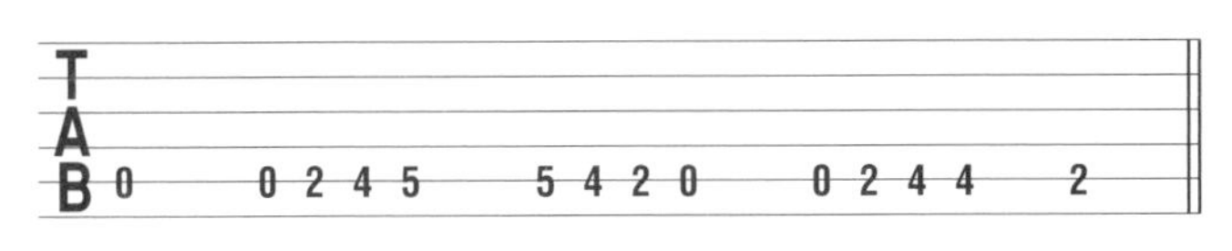




# RHYTHM TAB

**Rhythm tab** adds rhythmic values to the basic tab staff. Bar lines, which you've already seen in the chords section, divide music into **measures**. A **time signature** tells how many beats are in each measure and what kind of note is counted as one beat. In **4/4 time** ("four-four"), there are four beats in each measure, and a **quarter note** is counted as one beat. It has a vertical stem joined to the tab number.

## FEEL THE BEAT

Count "1, 2, 3, 4" as you play.

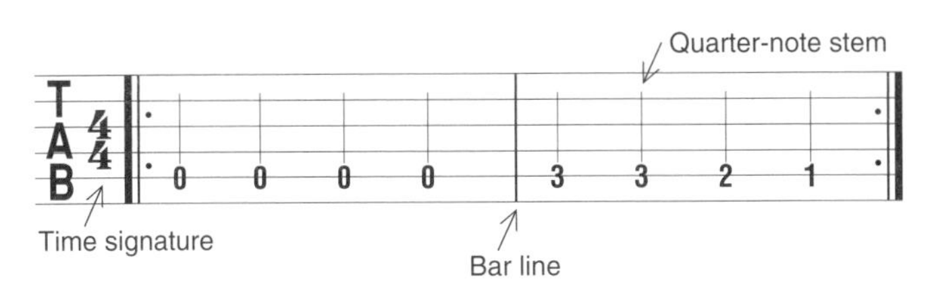




## OOM-PAH

This pattern often recalls the "oom-pah" sound of polka music, but as you'll learn later, it is also a common bass pattern for strumming chords.

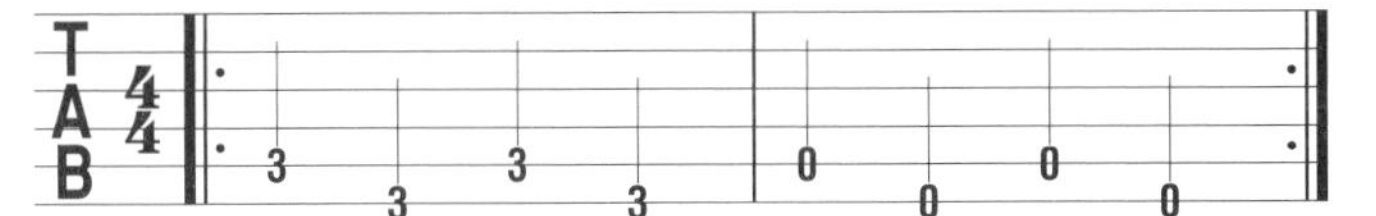

## BLUES RIFF

Use your fret hand's 3rd finger for notes on the 4th fret, 1st finger for the note on the 2nd fret, and 4th finger (pinky) for the note on the 5th fret.

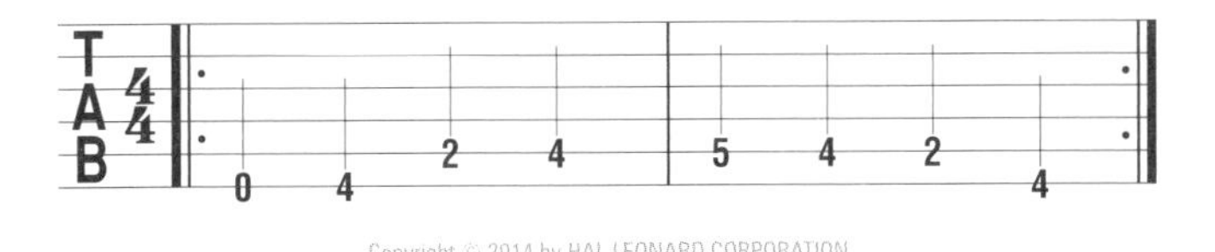




## ZEPPELIN TRIBUTE

Anchor the palm of your pick hand on the bridge of the guitar to help your picking accuracy.

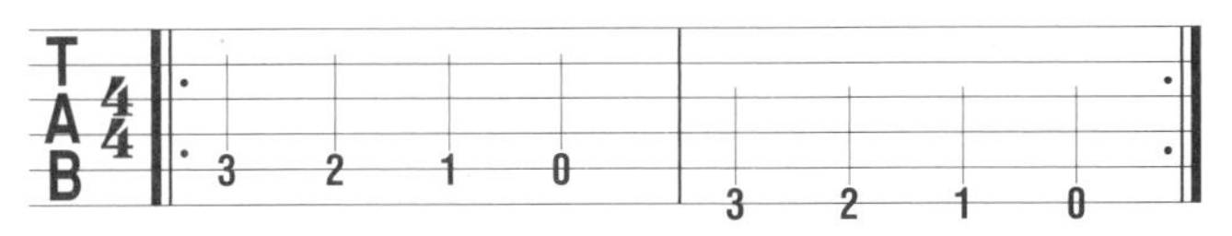

# MORE RIFFS

This next two riffs are written in **3/4 time**, which means there are three beats in each measure, and a quarter note receives one beat.

## MALAGUEÑA

This traditional Spanish piece is very popular among classical guitarists.

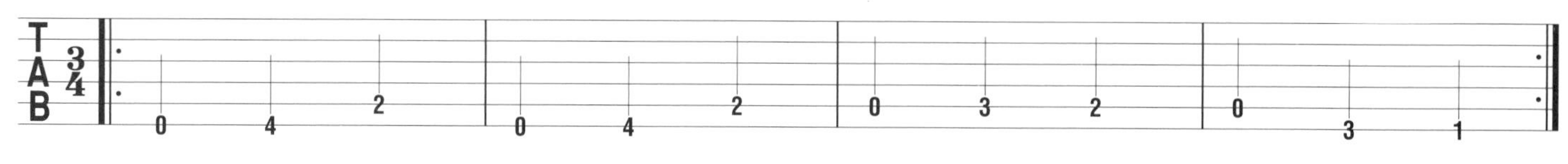


By Francisco Tarrega


## LEYENDA

Here is another popular classical piece, this time from Spanish composer Isaac Albeniz.

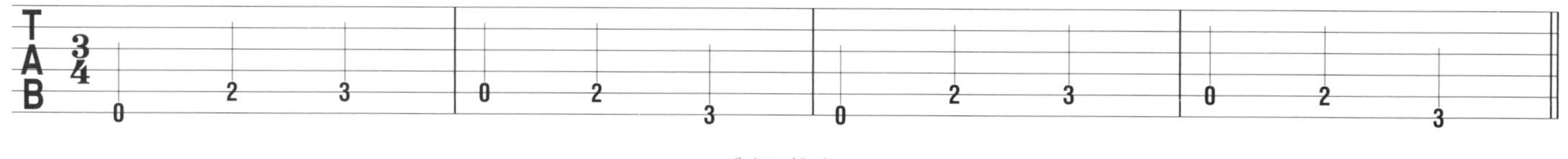


By Isaac Albeniz


A **half note** lasts two beats. It fills the time of two quarter notes. In tab, a circle surrounds the tab number(s) and is attached to a vertical stem.

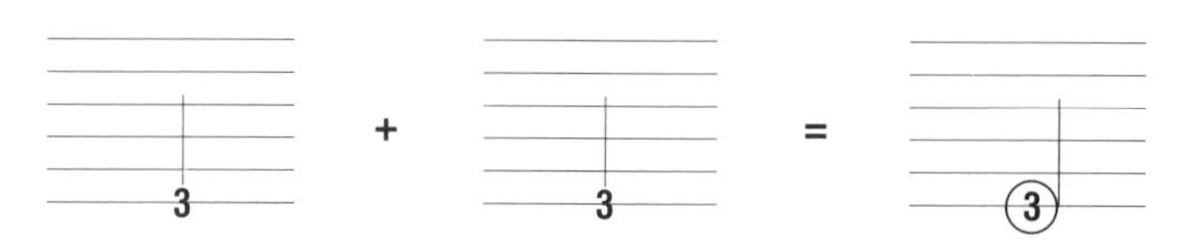


## CANON IN D

The first line is played with half notes and the second line is played with quarter notes. Count aloud and keep a steady tempo.

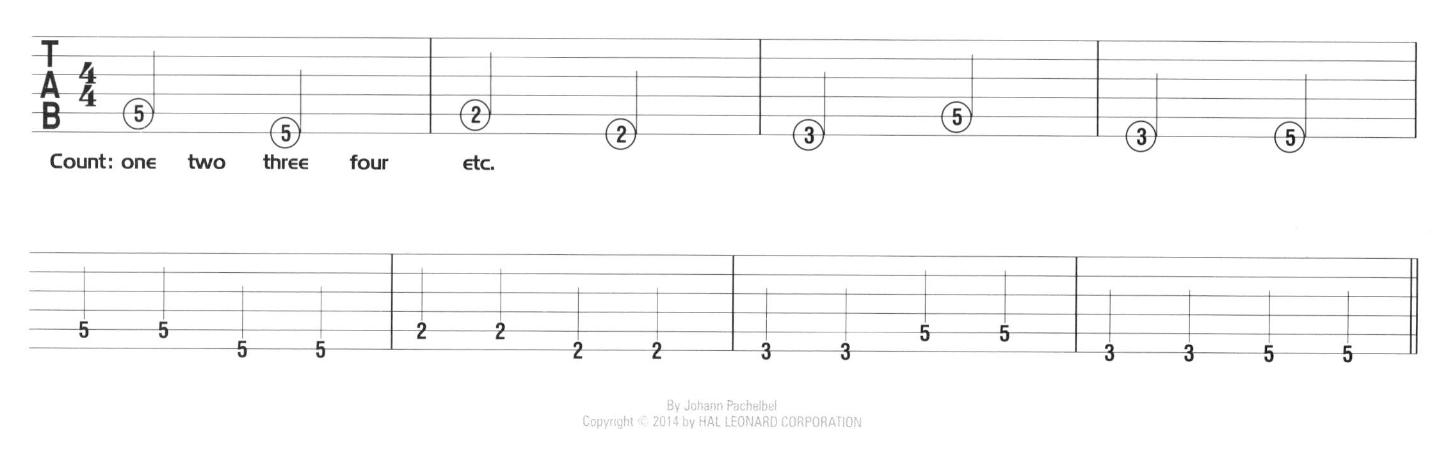


By Johann Pachelbel


## CHORD RIFF

This riff combines playing chords and single notes in 3/4 time. Remember to hold the half notes for two beats.

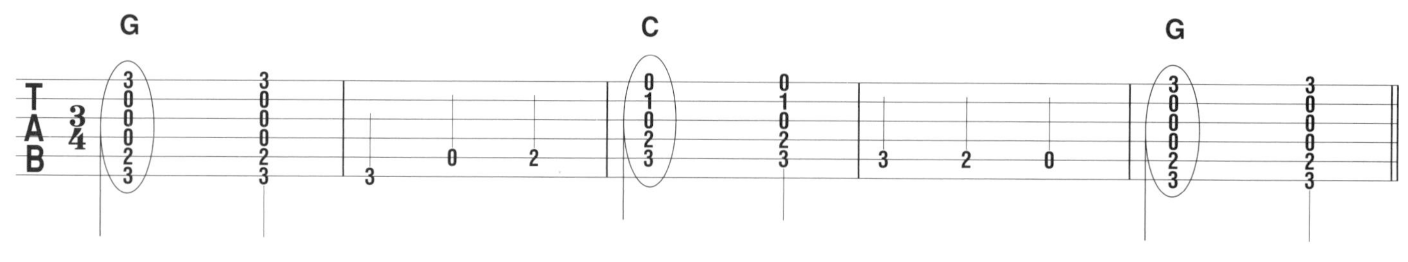

An **eighth note** lasts half a beat, or half as long as a quarter note. One eighth note is written with a stem and flag; consecutive eighth notes are connected with a beam.

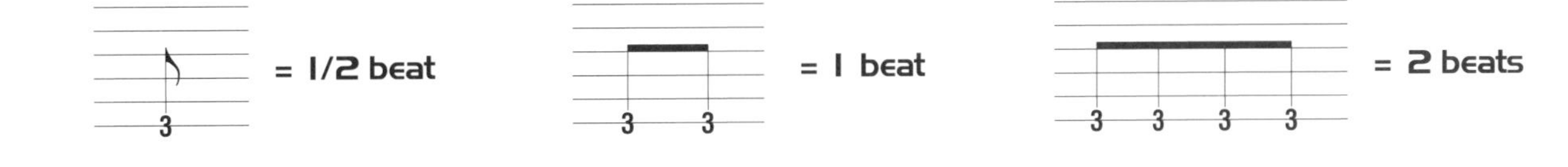


## LADY MADONNA

While playing this Beatles classic, count with the word "and" between the beats.

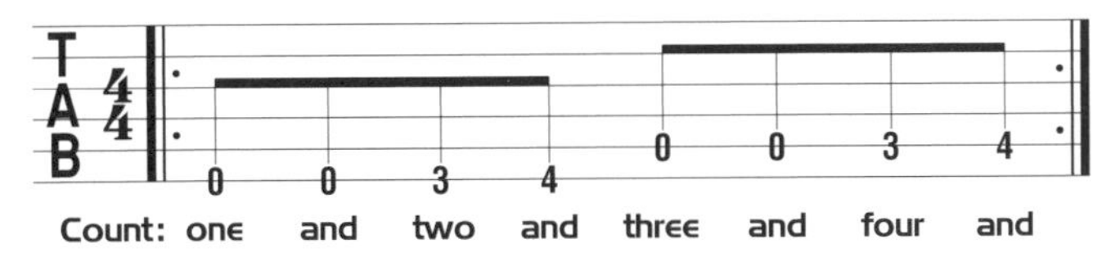




## COME AS YOU ARE

This Nirvana hit mixes eighth notes and quarter notes.

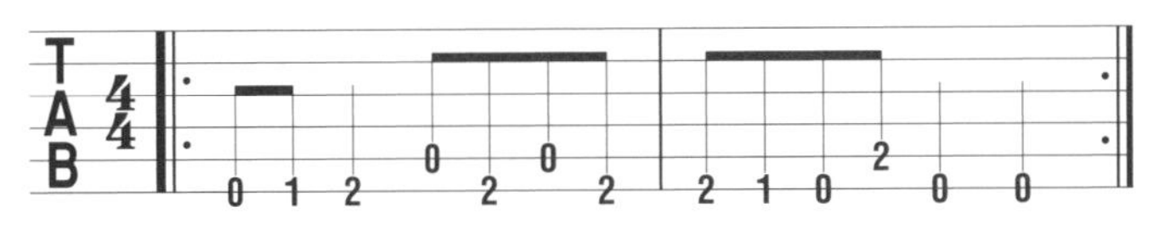



## LOVESONG

The bass line to this Cure song also mixes quarter and eighth notes. Be sure to use your fingertips; don't play "flat-fingered."

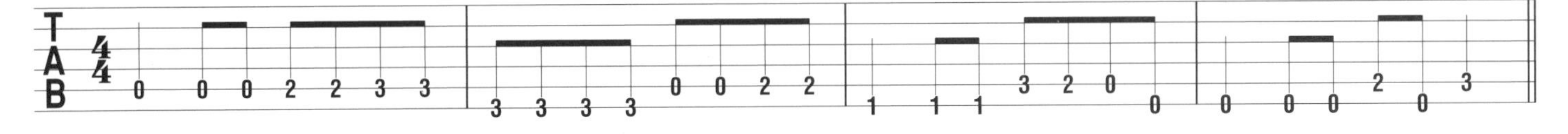

A **rest** is a symbol used to indicate silence in music. In 4/4 time, a **quarter rest** fills the time of one beat, and a **half rest** fills the time of two beats.

## 25 OR 6 TO 4

This riff by the band Chicago uses a quarter rest. Mute the string by touching it gently with the palm of your picking hand. You can also release the pressure of your fret hand to silence the string.

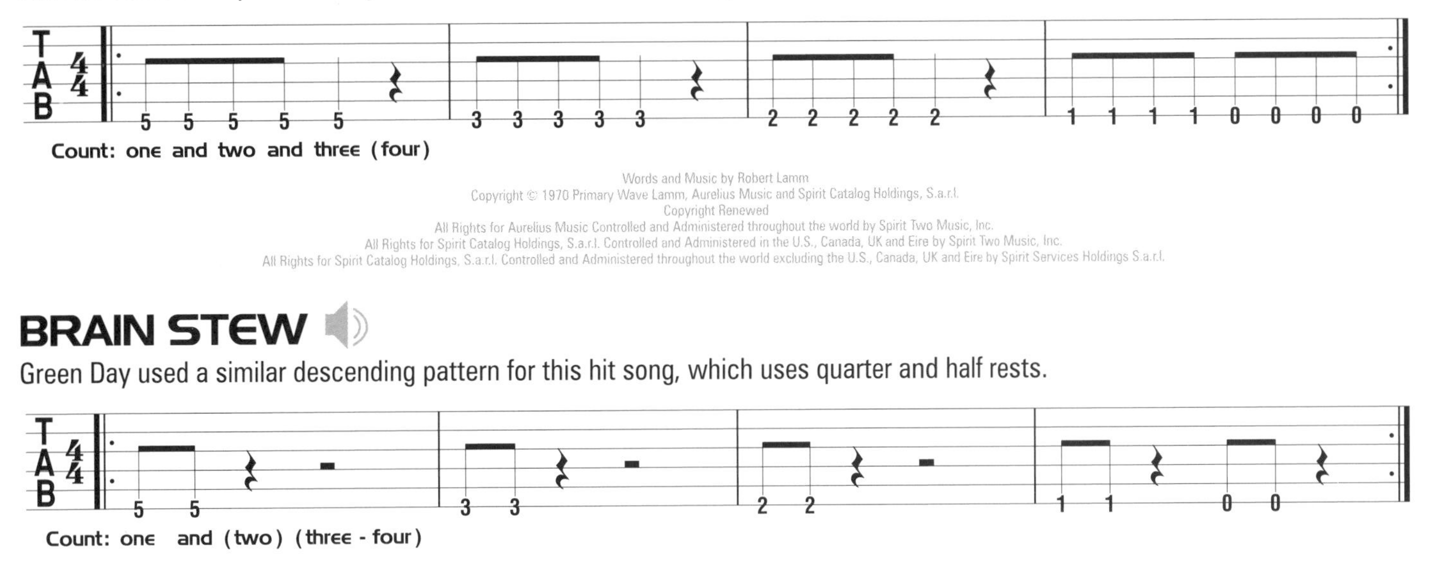




## BRAIN STEW

Green Day used a similar descending pattern for this hit song, which uses quarter and half rests.

# THE D STRING

Here are the notes within the first five frets of the 4th string, called the D string.

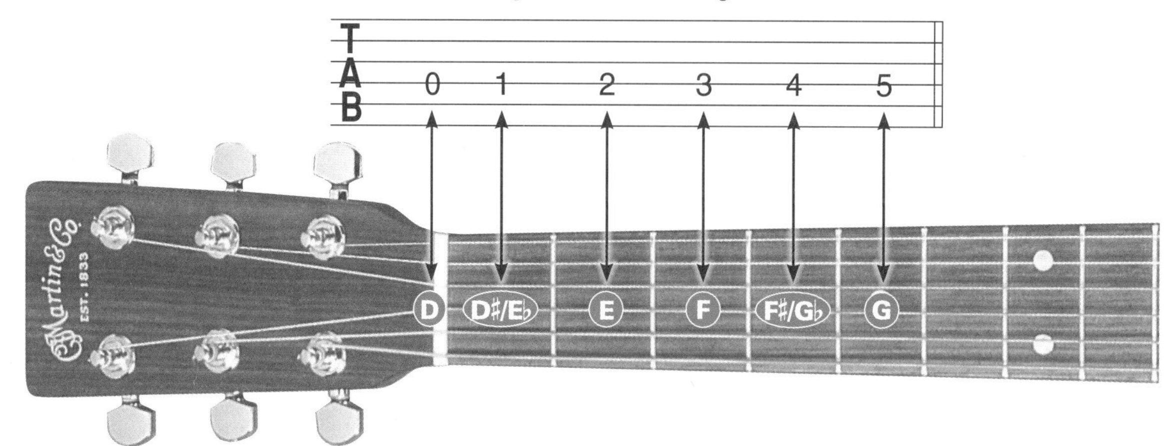


## GOT D BLUES

Practice notes on the D string with this classic blues riff.

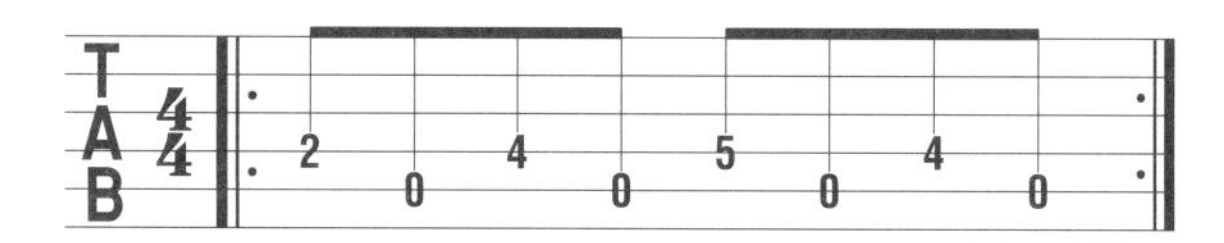




## OH, PRETTY WOMAN

This Roy Orbison song features one of most recognizable riffs of all time.

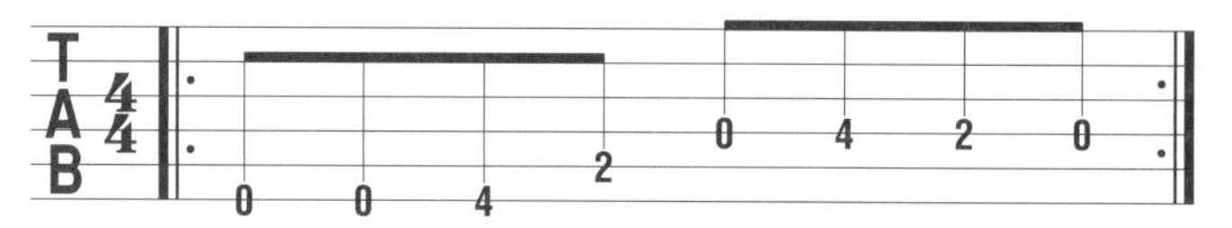




## THE JOKER

The riff in this Steve Miller Band classic is certainly no joke, but rather a fun ditty played on the bottom three strings. Watch for those quarter rests.

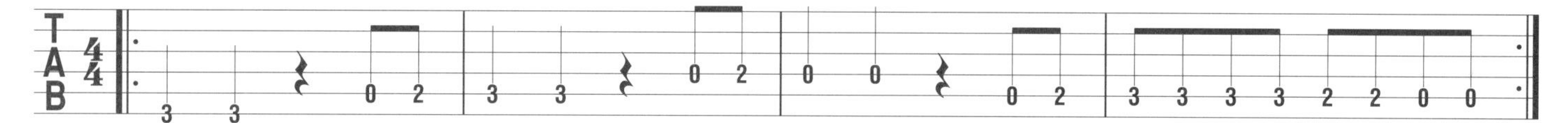




A **tie** is a curved, dashed line connecting two notes—or chords—of the same pitch. It tells you not to strike the second note. The first note should be struck and held for the combined value of both notes.

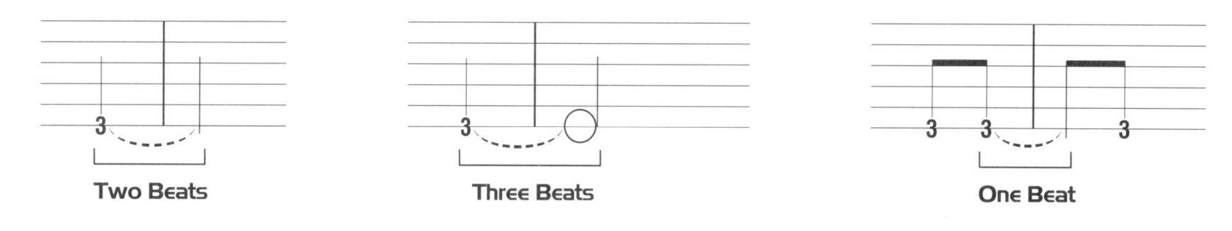


## I CAN'T HELP MYSELF (SUGAR PIE, HONEY BUNCH)

Now you're ready to tackle this Motown classic by the Four Tops.

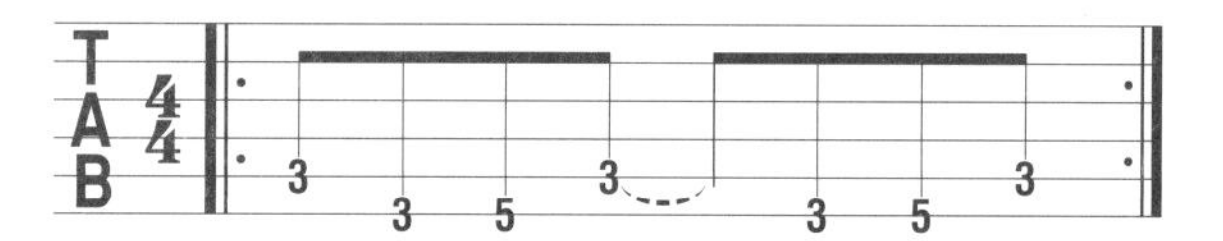




## MONEY (THAT'S WHAT I WANT)

Countless artists, including Barrett Strong, the Beatles, Buddy Guy, and Waylon Jennings, have recorded "Money."

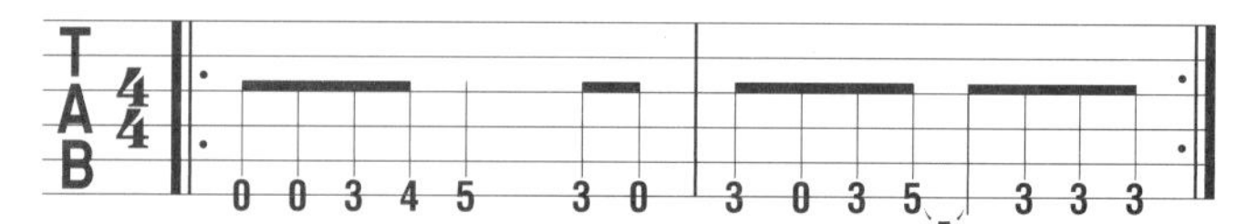

## WAGON WHEEL

This hit for Darius Rucker and Old Crow Medicine Show uses all four chords you've learned so far along with a couple of ties.

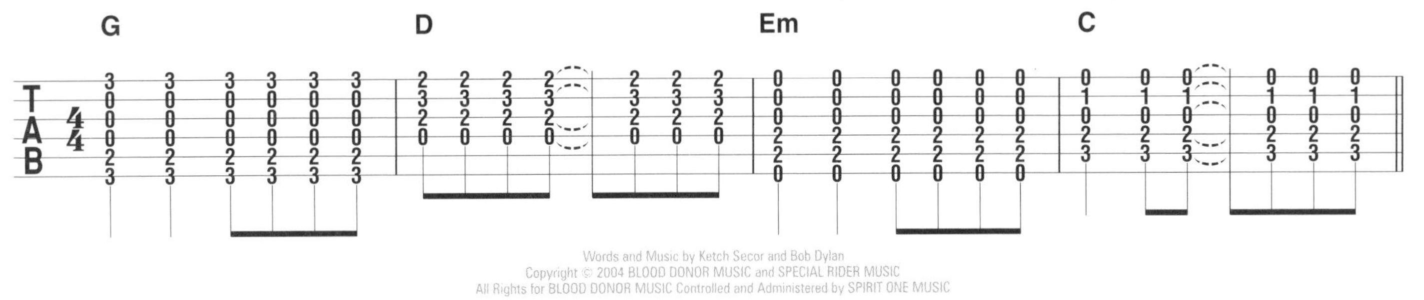




## HEART OF GOLD

For the verse of this Neil Young classic, you'll combine single notes on the E, A, and D strings with strummed chords.

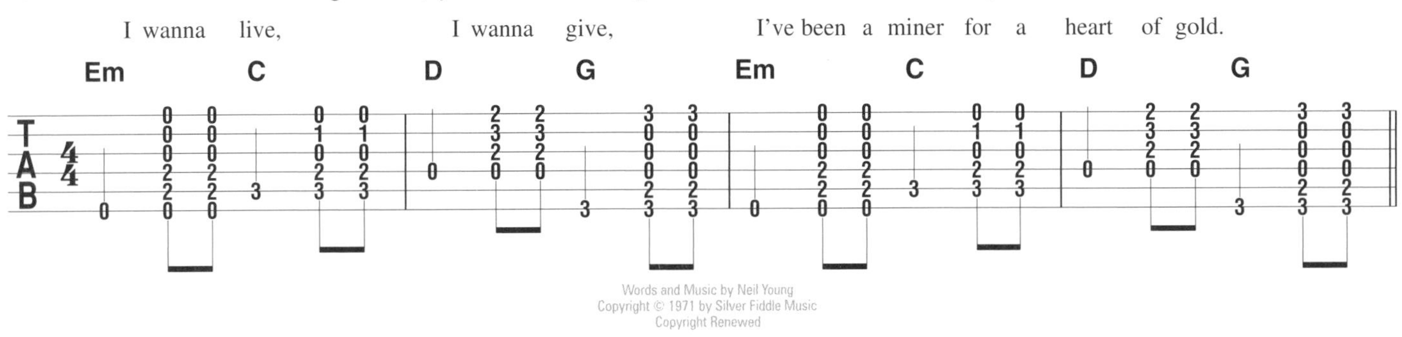




An **eighth rest** indicates to be silent for half a beat. It looks like this: 𝄾

## HAVA NAGILA

Start slowly and use your pinky for the G♯ on the 4th fret.

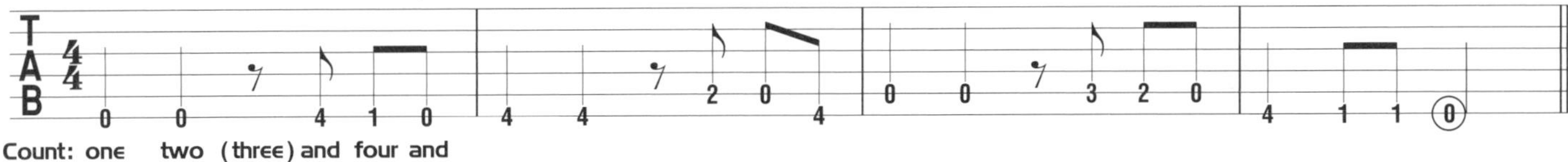




## DAY TRIPPER

On this Beatles classic, you'll get a workout on all three bottom strings.

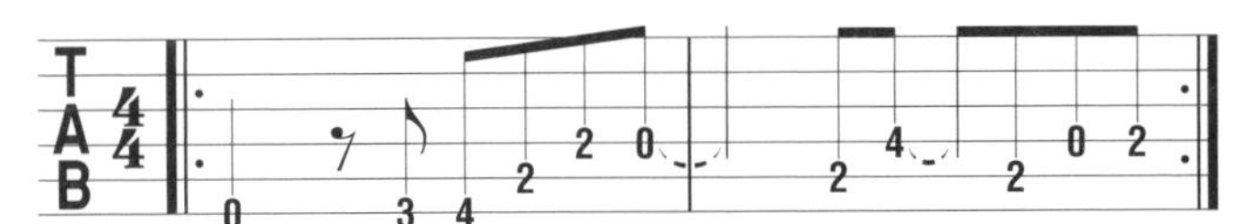




## SHOULD I STAY OR SHOULD I GO

This Clash classic combines rests and chord strums.

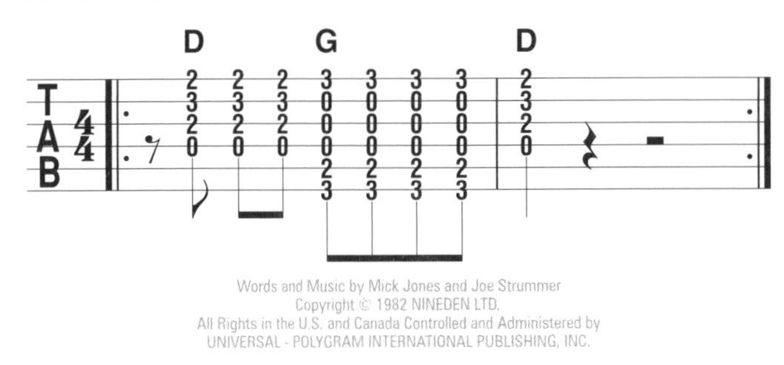




## PINK HOUSES

This next riff begins with a **pickup note**. Count the pickup note as if it was the last portion of a full measure.

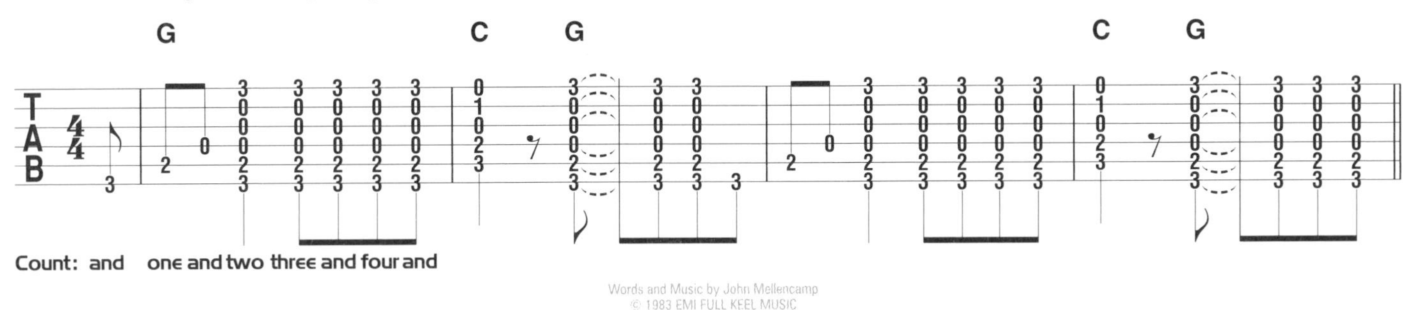

## GOOD RIDDANCE (TIME OF YOUR LIFE)

Now it's time to play another full song. Green Day's "Good Riddance" has become one of the most popular acoustic strummers of the past 20 years. It's presented here with three strum patterns essential to acoustic guitar.

The final chord of the song should ring for the full measure. This is called a **whole note**, which is twice as long as a half note and is written in a circle with no stem.

Intro

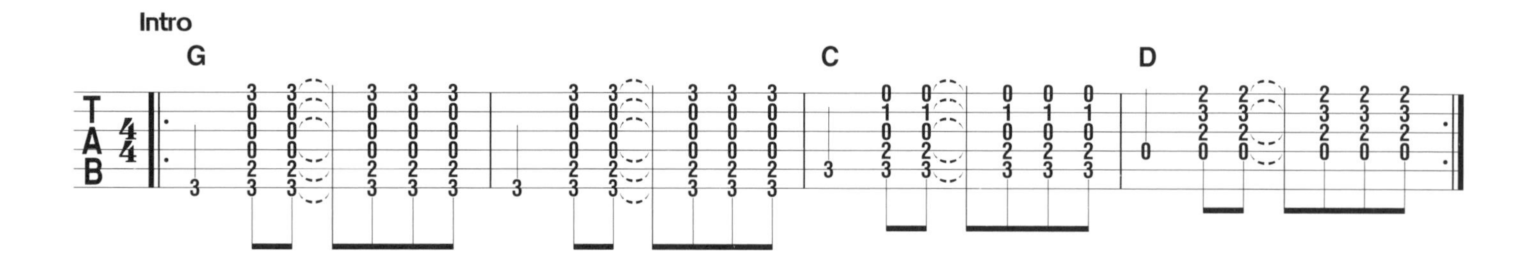


Verse

1. Another turning point, a fork stuck in the road.
2. So take the photographs and still frames in your mind.

G C D

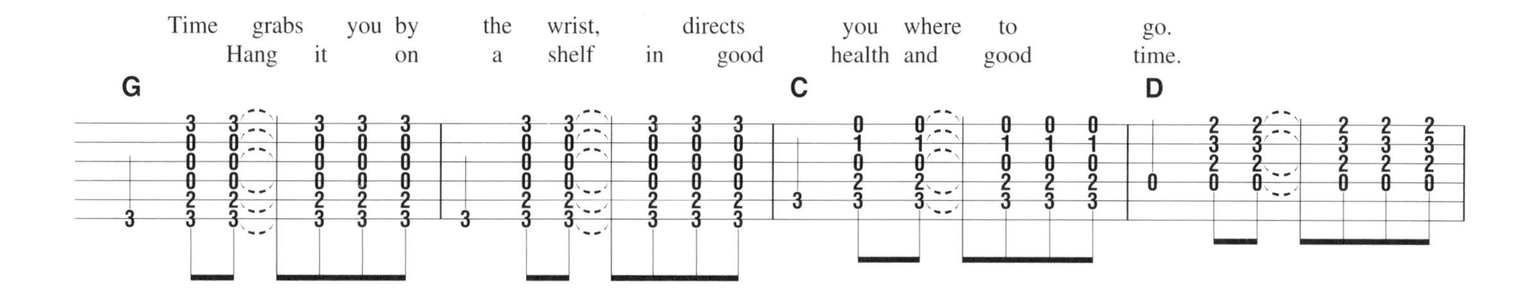


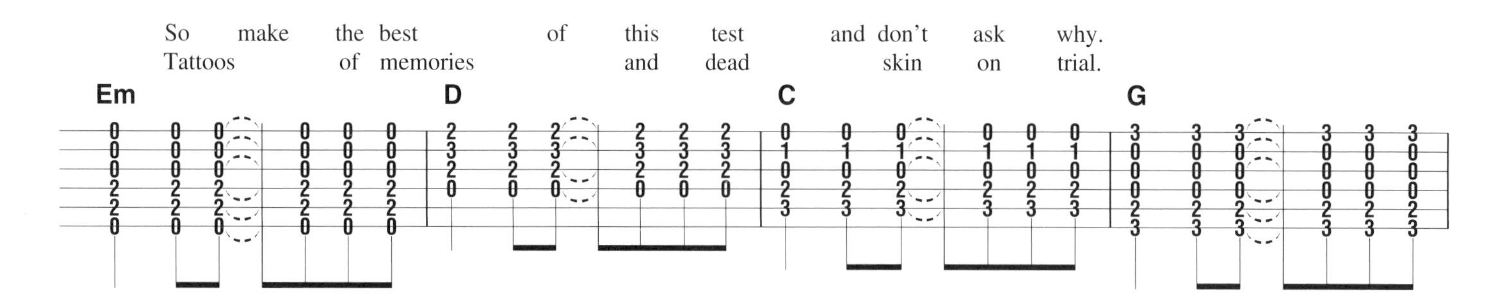

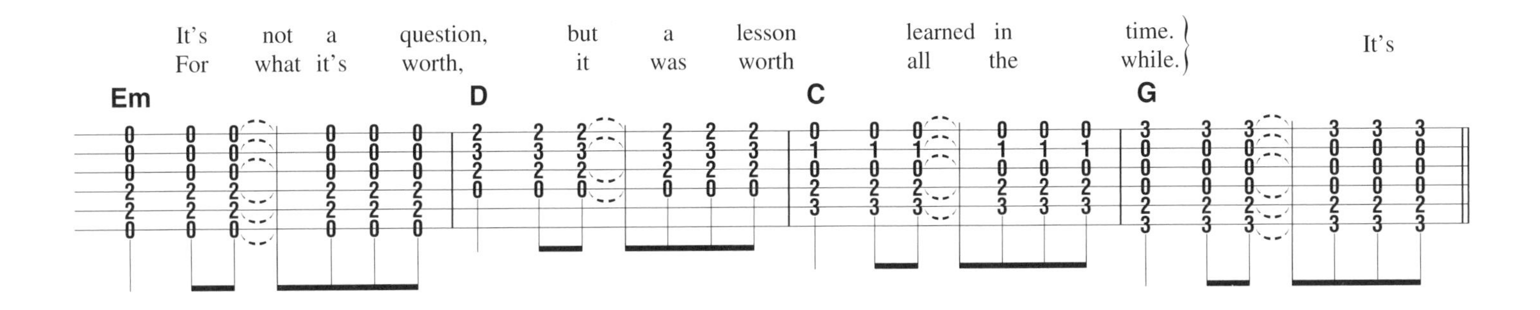
It's not a question, but a lesson learned in time.
For what it's worth, it was worth all the while.
It's
Em
D
C
G

## Chorus

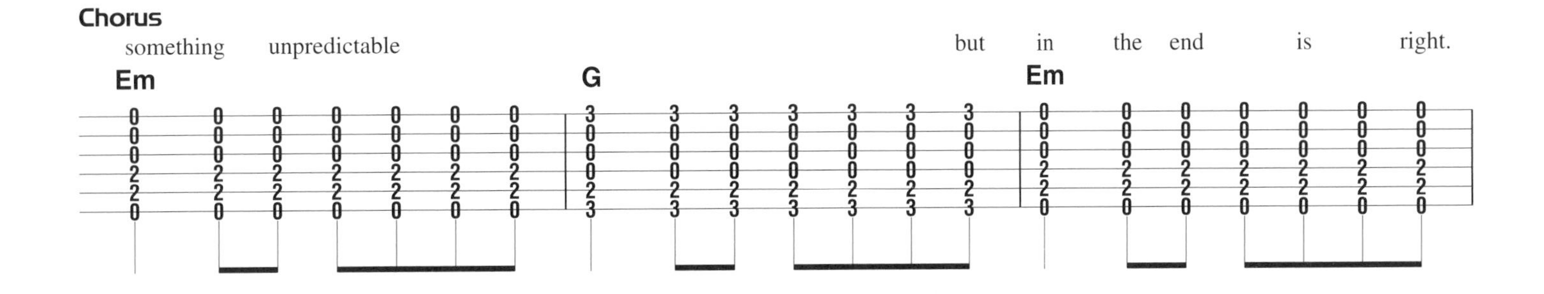
something unpredictable but in the end is right.
Em
G
Em

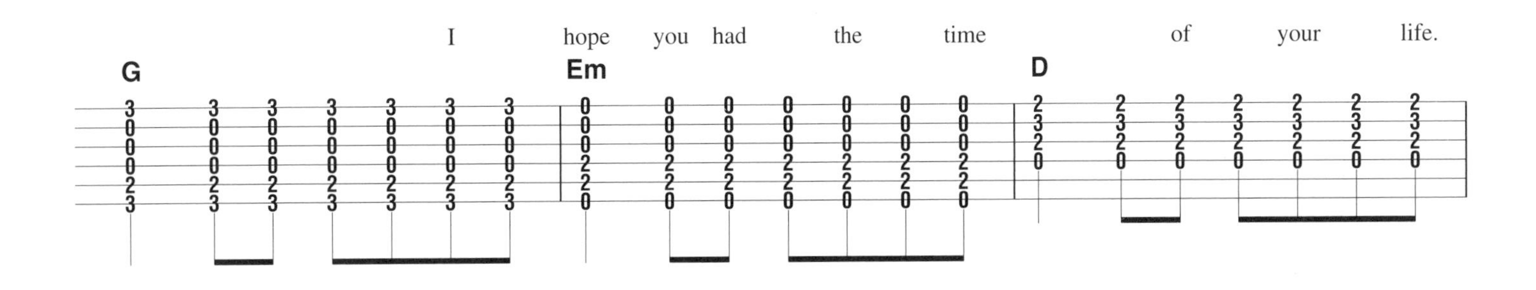
I hope you had the time of your life.
G
Em
D

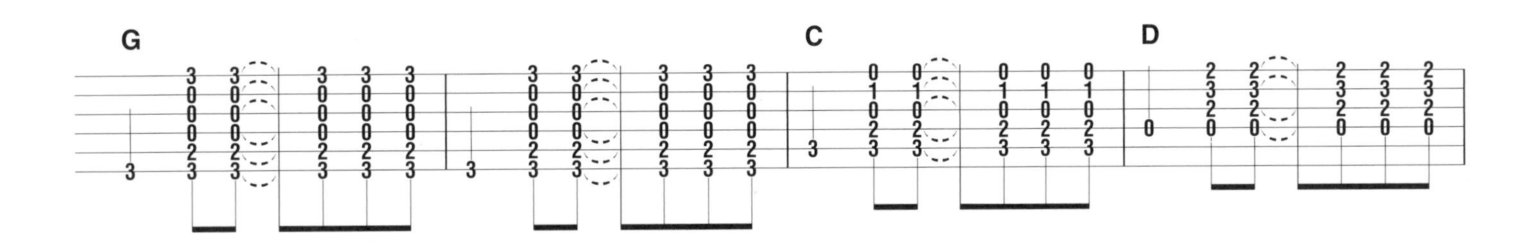
G
C
D

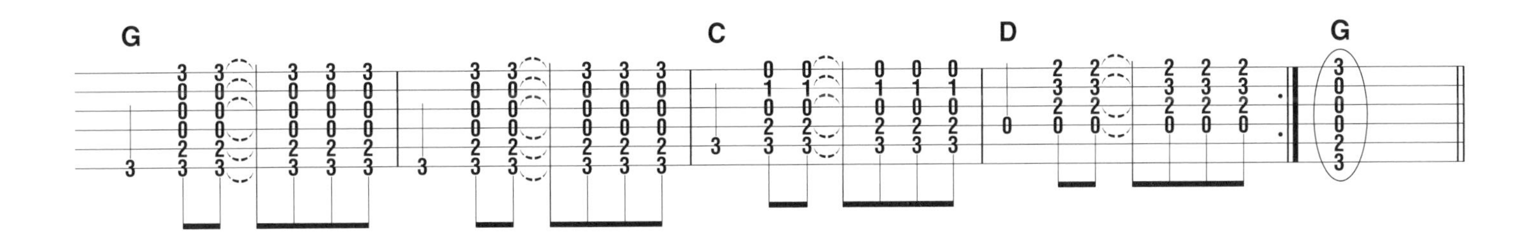
G
C
D
G

## WIPE OUT

Now let's try a single-note workout on the bottom three strings. "Wipe Out" is one of the most popular instrumental hits of all time. It was originally recorded by the Surfaris in 1963 and since has been performed by numerous groups, including the Ventures and the Beach Boys.

During the famous drum breakdown in the second half of the song, you'll notice a **whole rest.** It indicates one full measure of silence and looks like this: ▬

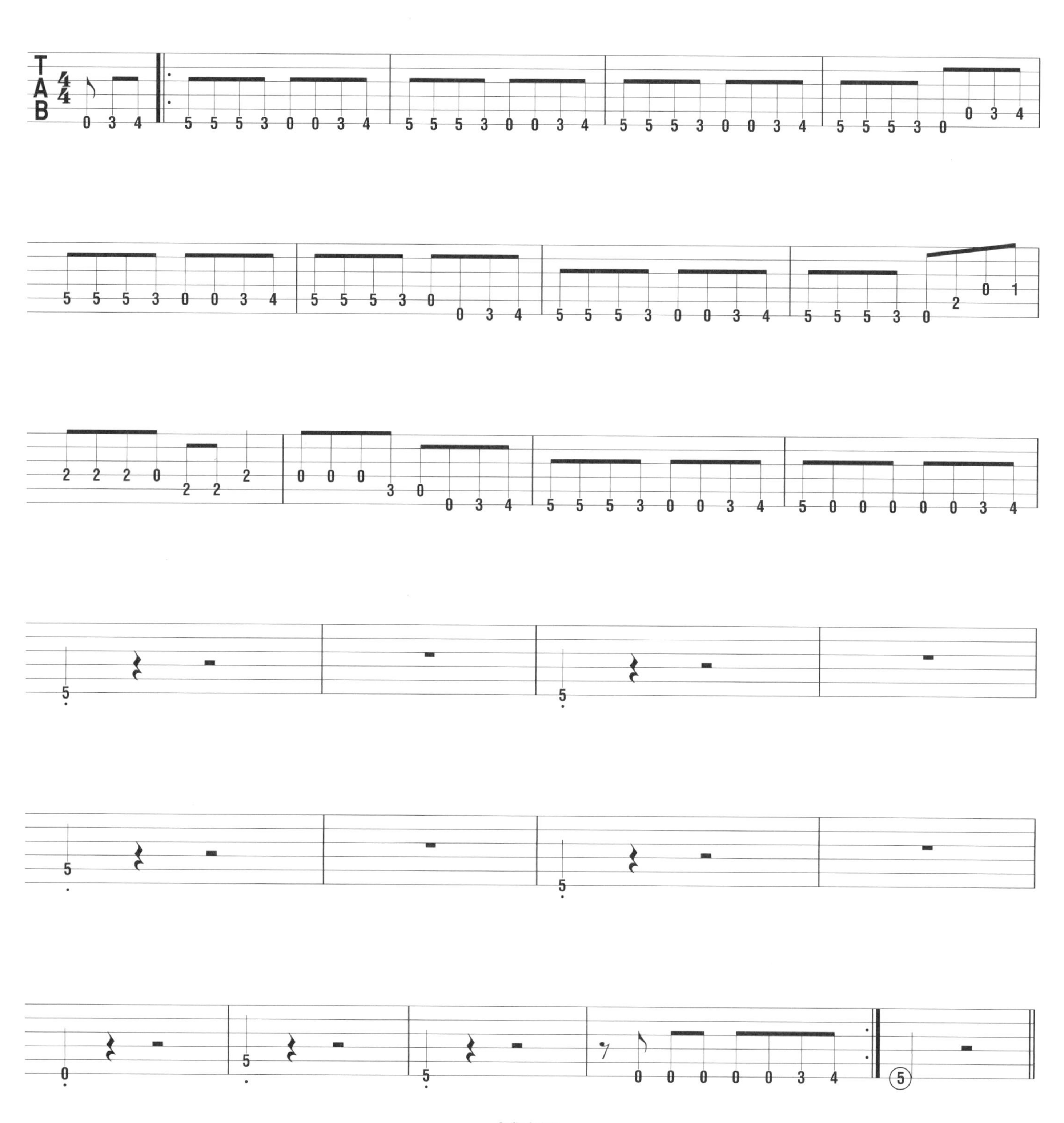

By The Surfaris

# CHECKPOINT

You're just over halfway through this book and well on your way to a rewarding hobby or a successful career with the guitar. Let's take a moment to review some of what you've learned so far.

## NOTE NAMES

Draw a line to match each note on the left with its correct name on the right.

## SYMBOLS & TERMS

Draw a line to match each symbol on the left with its correct name on the right.

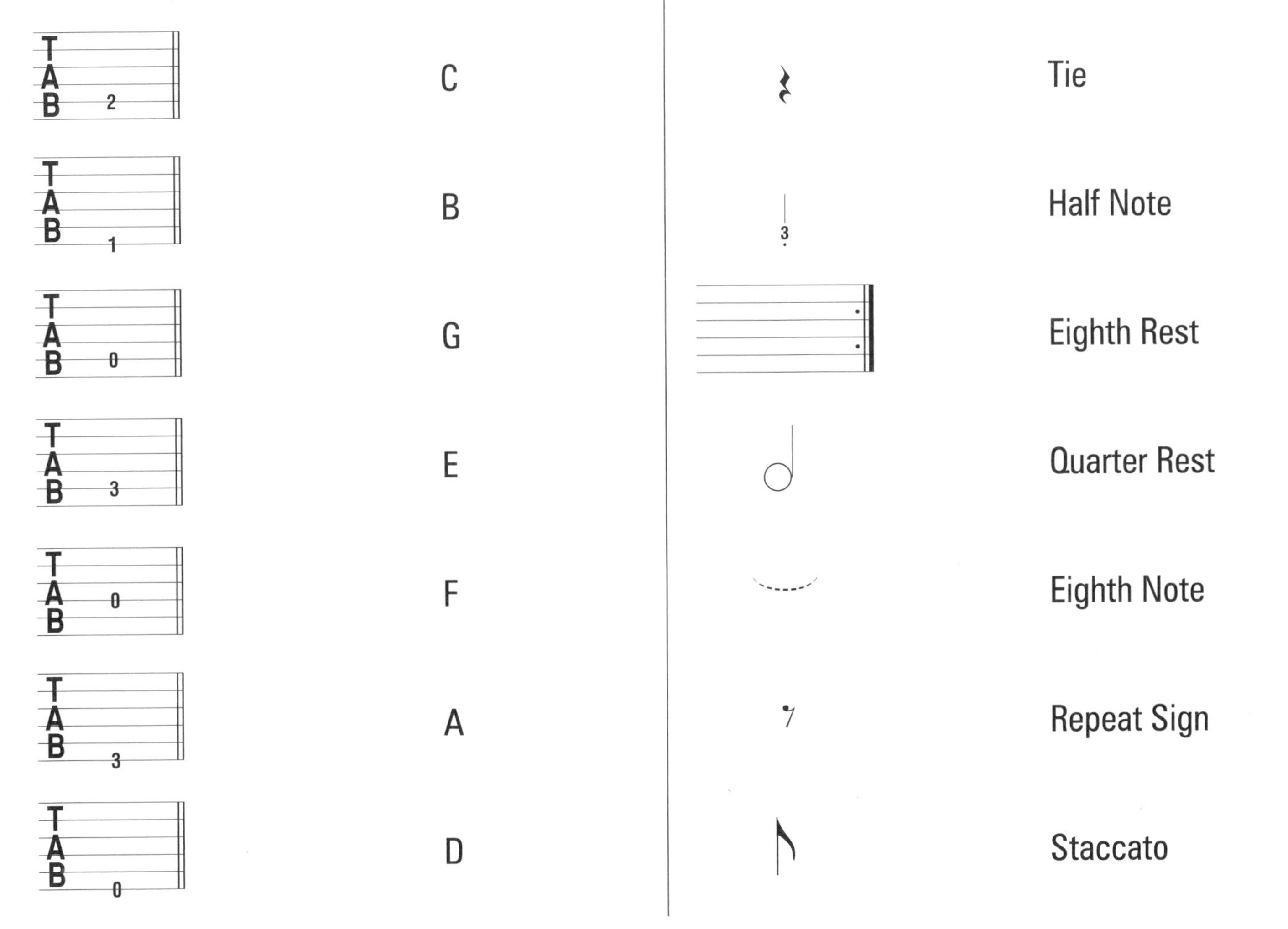


Write the note names in the spaces provided.

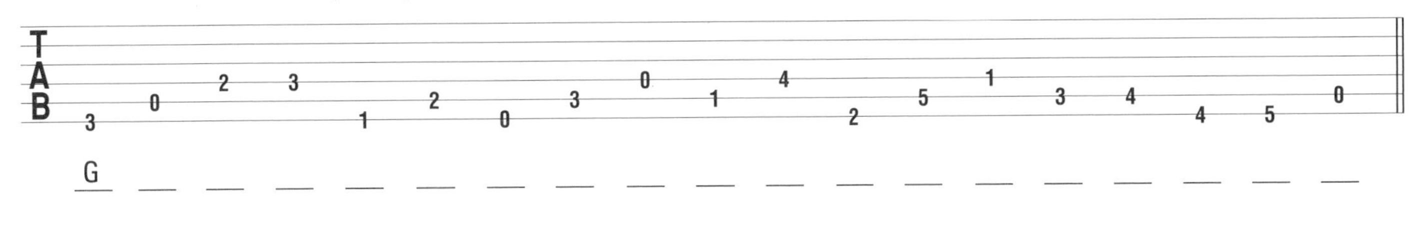


Add bar lines.

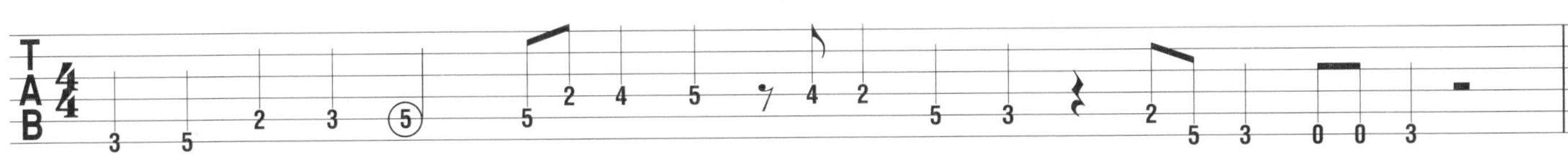

Below the tab staff are note names. Write the notes on the tab staff.

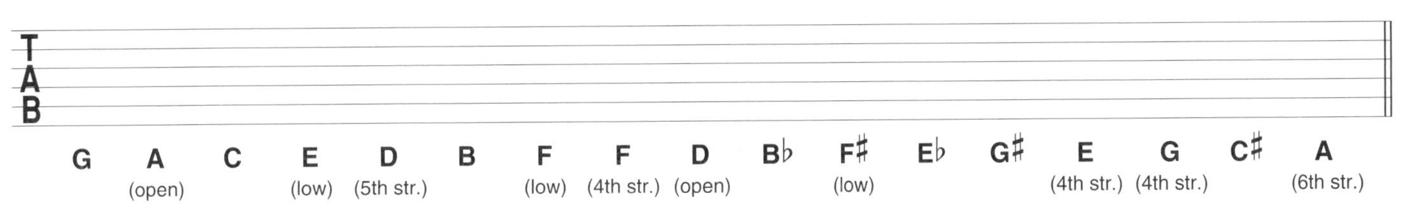

# NEW CHORDS

Here are two new chords: A minor and D minor.

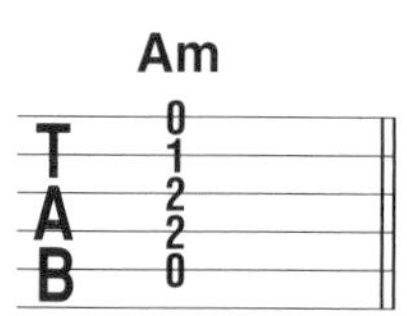


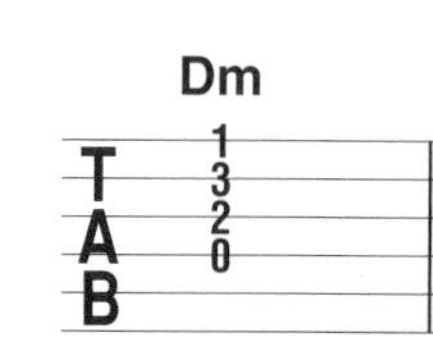

## A FEW MINOR CHANGES

This progression features all three minor chords you've learned so far. It also features each chord root played as a single note. A **root note** is the note upon which the chord is named.

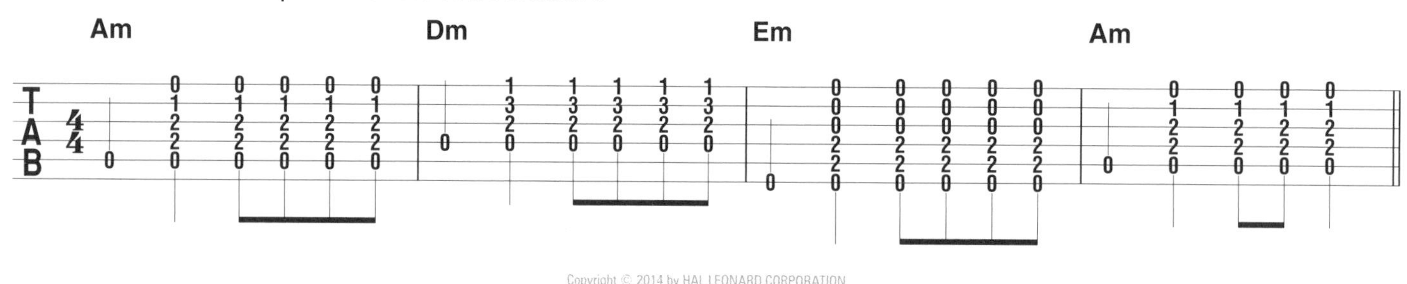




## BETH

Kiss drummer Peter Criss composed this classic ballad on the piano, but it also sounds beautiful on a strummed acoustic guitar. Here's the intro.

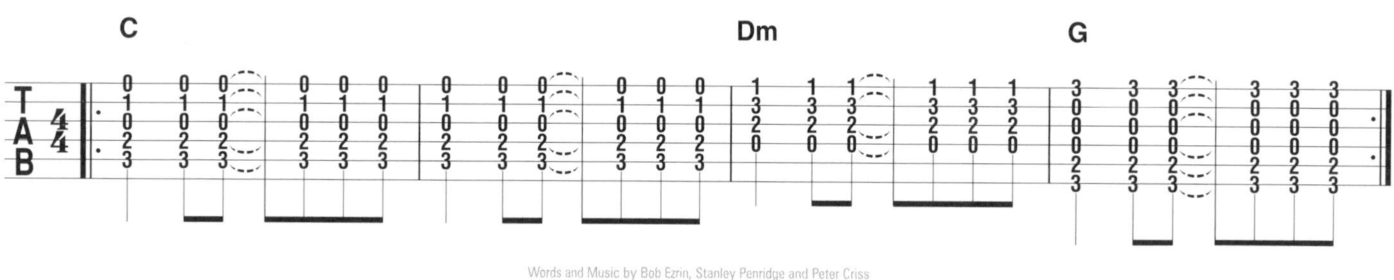




## CLOCKS

Another classic piano riff, Coldplay's "Clocks" introduces the **accent**, which means you should strum the indicated chords slightly louder than the others. The accent symbol looks like this: >

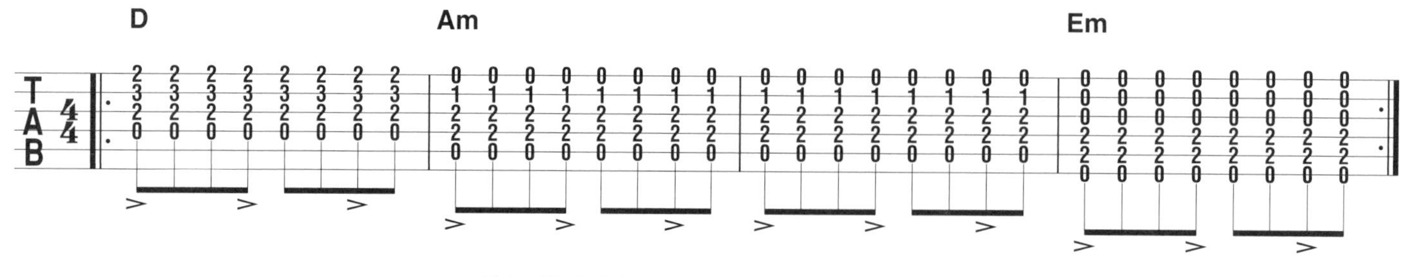

# KNOCKIN' ON HEAVEN'S DOOR

Bob Dylan's timeless ballad features the Am chord and offers a review of the G, C, and D chords. Follow the strumming rhythms as notated or just read the chord symbols and improvise your own strum patterns.

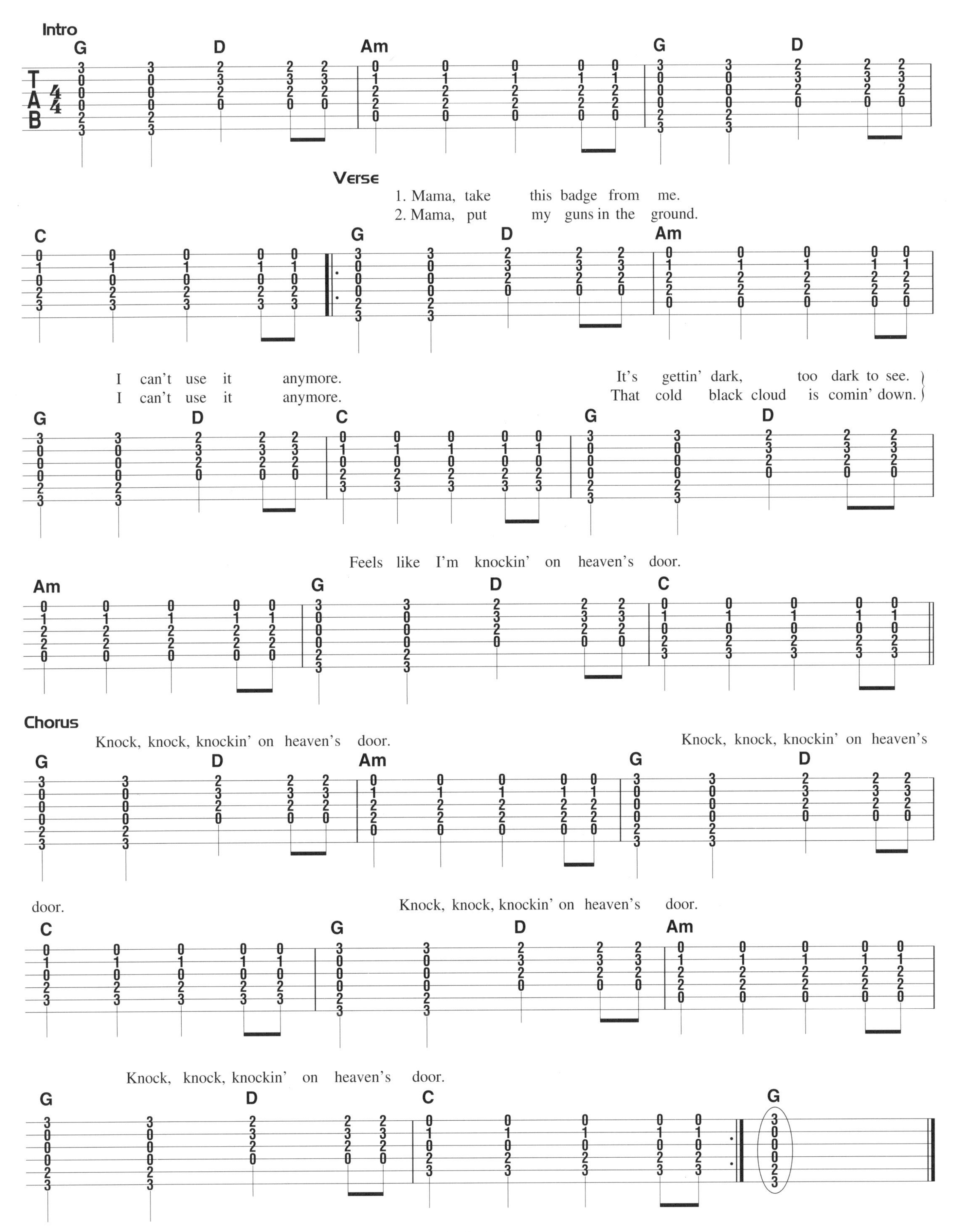

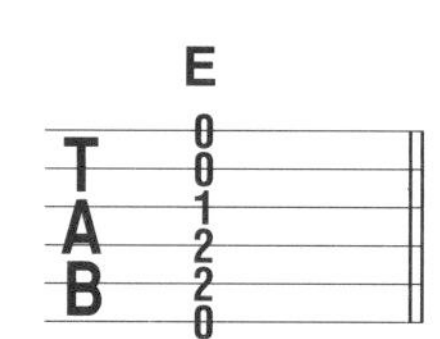


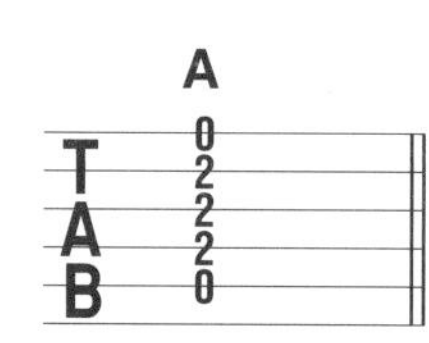


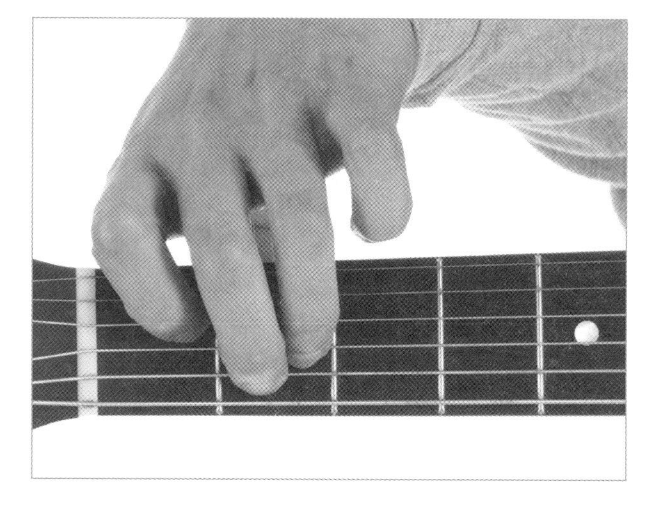

## ABOUT A GIRL

For songs that change chords quickly, like this one by Nirvana, it's OK to release your fingers from one chord early to arrive at the next chord on time. It's natural for a few open strings to be struck in transition.

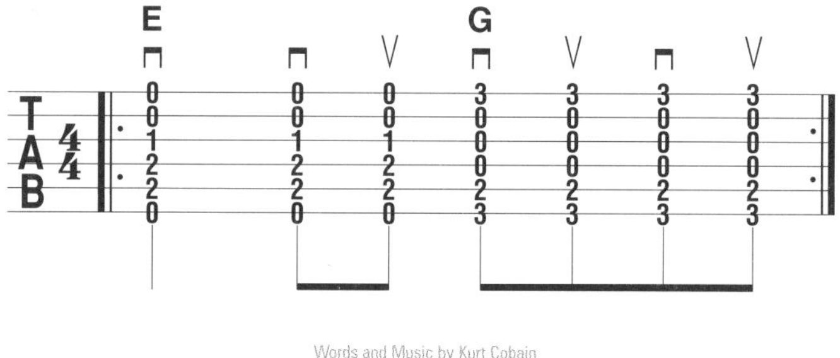




## SOUTHERN CROSS

This Crosby, Stills & Nash classic incorporates a single B note. If you find that too difficult, just strum the D chord twice.

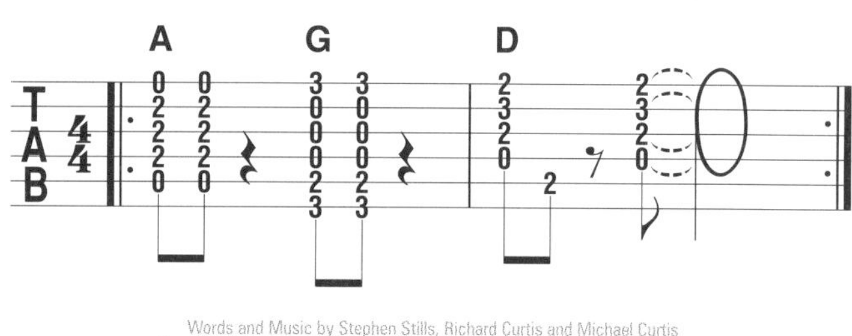




## BYE BYE LOVE

Another way to play an A chord is to lay your 1st finger across the three fretted strings at the 2nd fret, allowing that same finger to mute the high E string. Experiment and choose which version works best for you in this hit by the Everly Brothers.

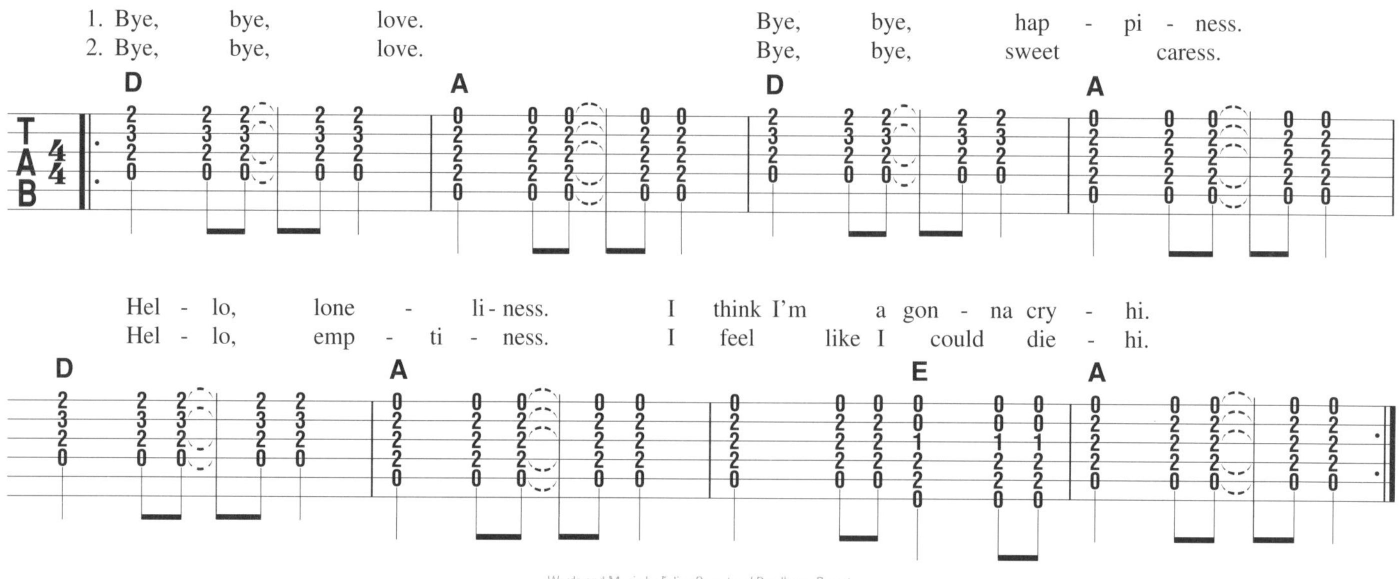

# PATIENCE

Here's a hit song by Guns N' Roses that uses five open chords.

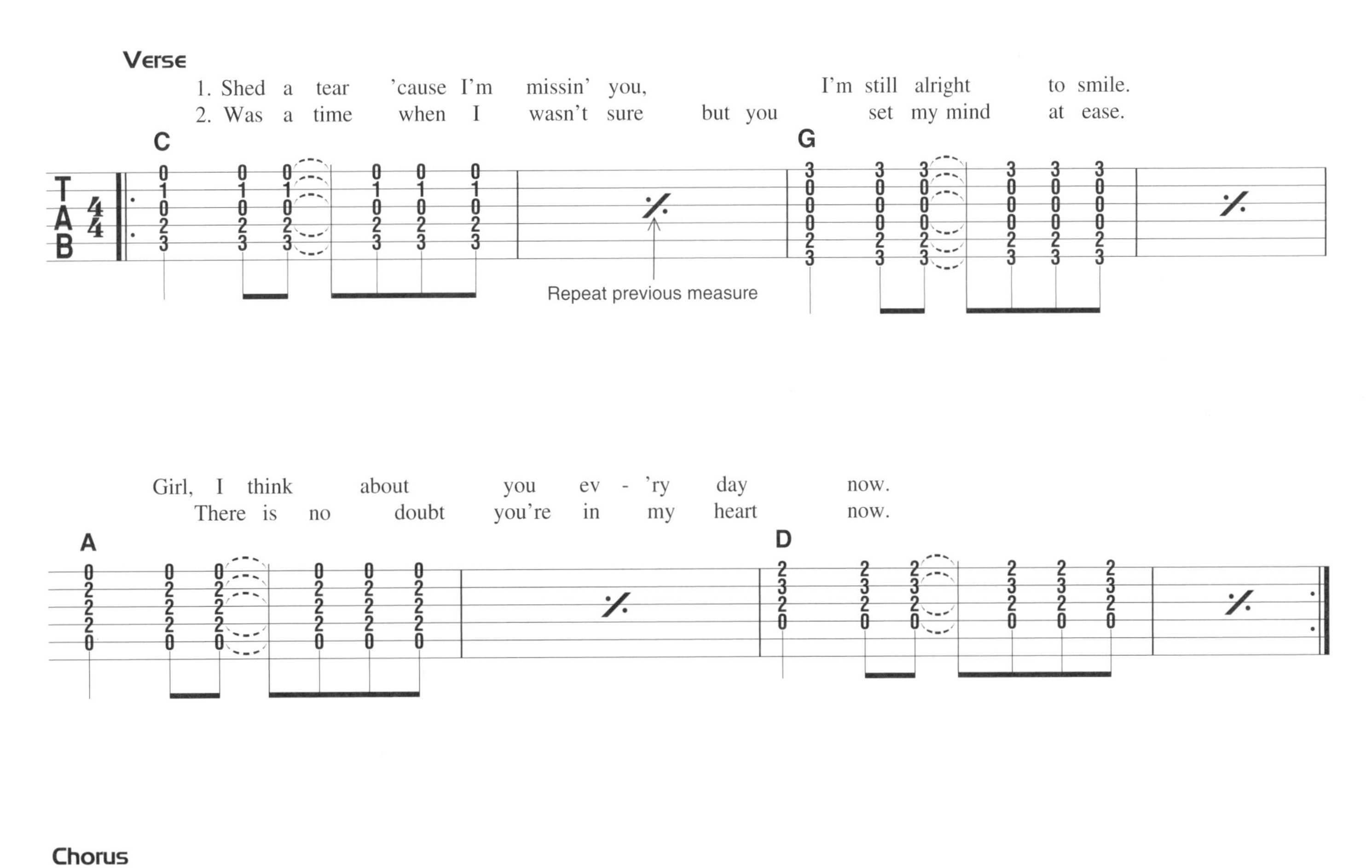


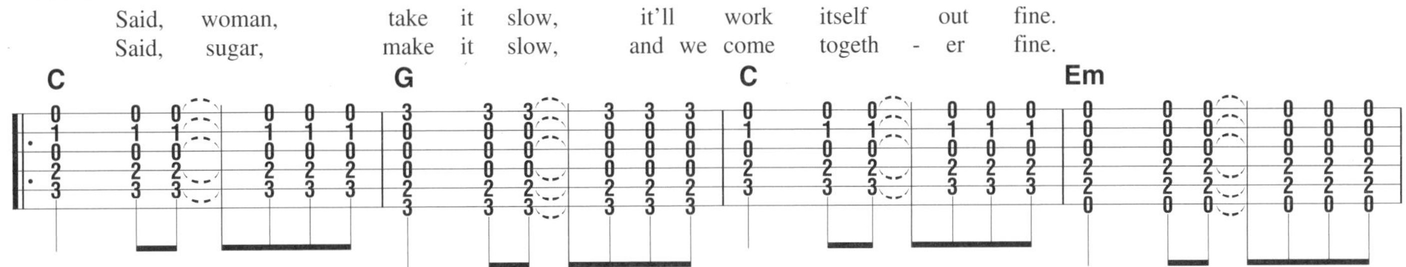


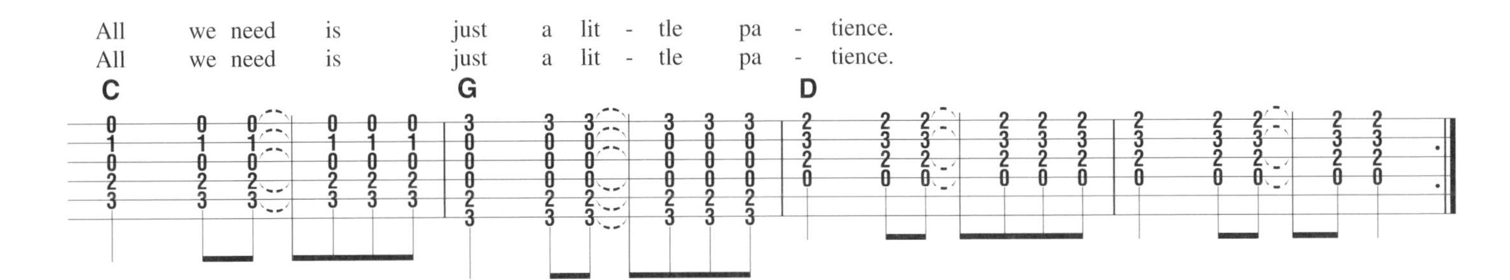

# THE G STRING

Here are the notes within the first five frets of the 3rd string, called the G string.

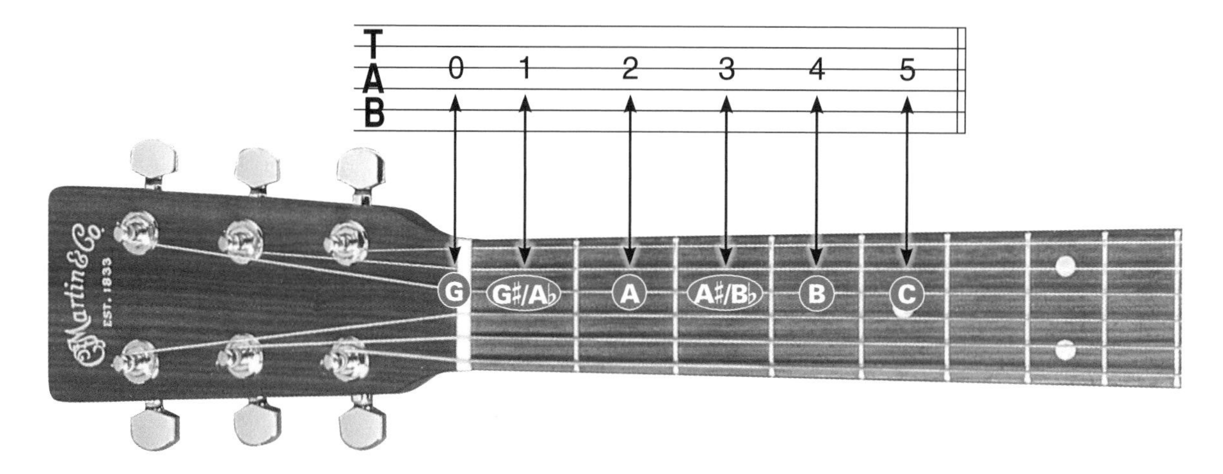


## NORWEGIAN WOOD (THIS BIRD HAS FLOWN)

This Indian-influenced Beatles song, written in 3/4 time, was the first rock song to feature a sitar on a recording.

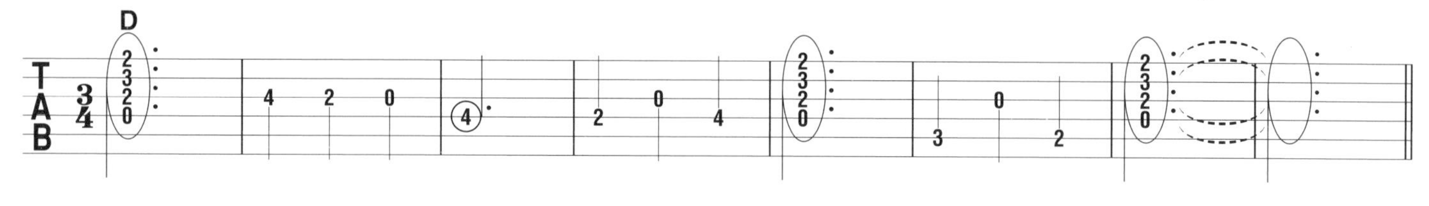




## DON'T FEAR THE REAPER

In some songs, like this cowbell-infused classic by Blue Öyster Cult, it's common to see the instruction "**let ring**." Instead of releasing your fingers after each note is played, you hold them down, allowing the notes to sustain.

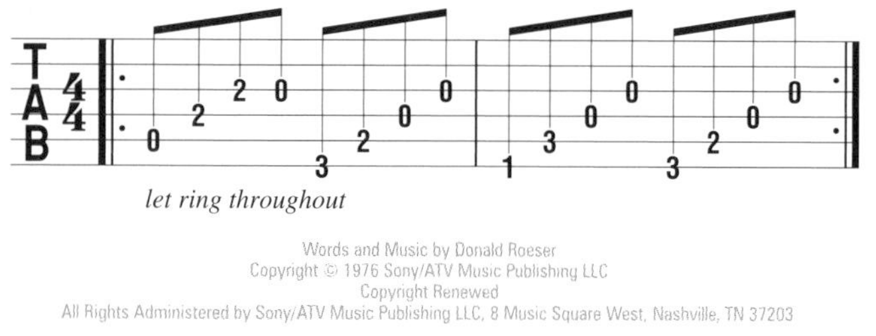




## LA BAMBA

This song has been recorded by Ritchie Valens, Los Lobos, and many others. It uses notes on all four strings you've learned so far. Use your 2nd finger to press the notes on the 2nd fret and 3rd finger on the 3rd fret.

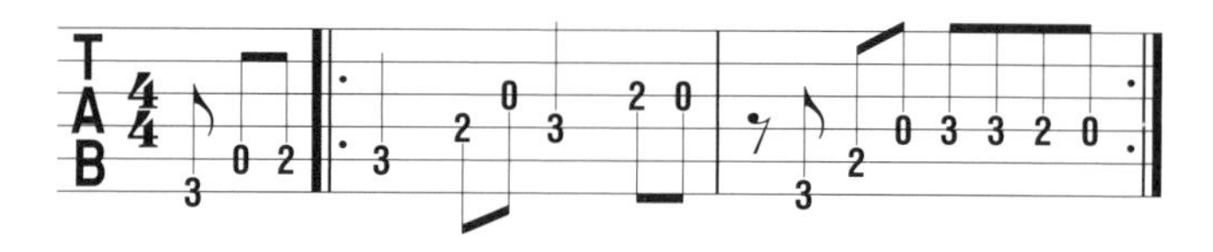




## SMOKE ON THE WATER

Deep Purple's "Smoke on the Water" features one of the greatest rock riffs of all time. Play the two-note chords, or **double stops** (sometimes called "dyads"), with downstrokes. Although you haven't learned notes beyond the 5th fret, use your 3rd finger to press the notes on the 6th fret.

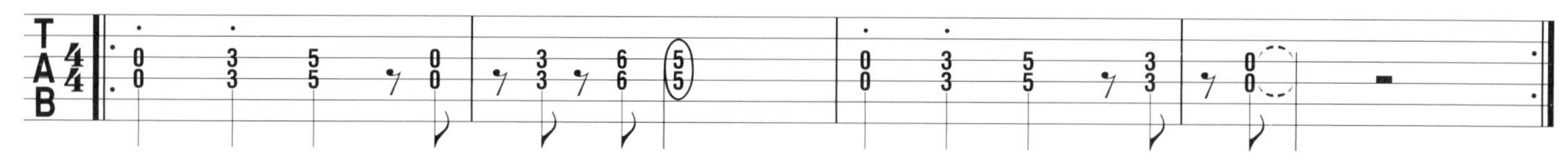

# THE B STRING

Here are the notes within the first five frets of the 2nd string, called the B string.

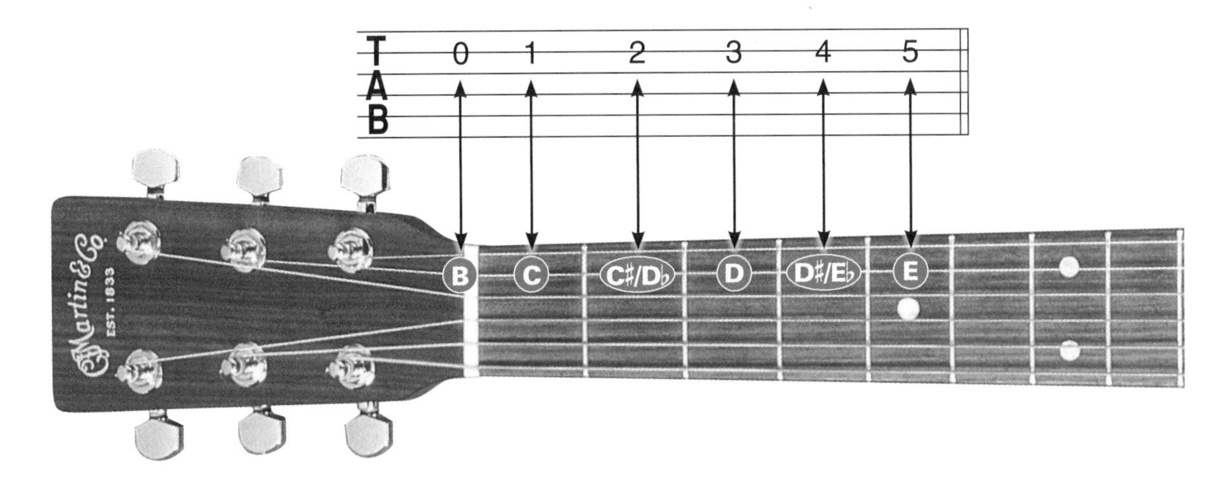


## DUELIN' BANJOS

This famous bluegrass theme was featured in the movie *Deliverance.*



## SUSIE-Q

Creedence Clearwater Revival covered this Dale Hawkins song on their first album.

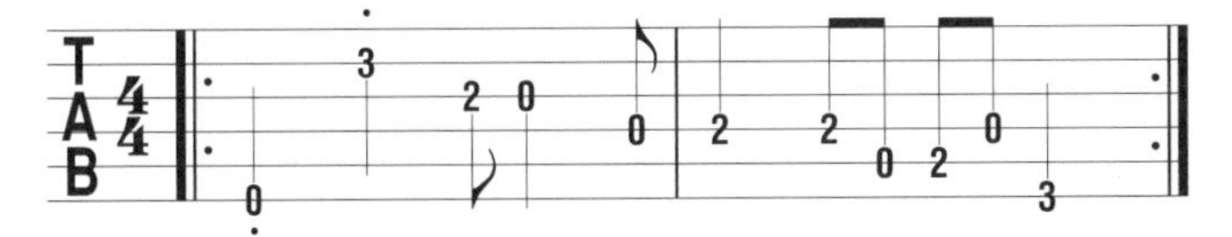



## FÜR ELISE

This instantly recognizable Beethoven piece in 3/4 time is truly a classic. The **ending brackets** above the tab staff indicate that when you play the melody the first time, you should use the 1st ending and repeat as usual. The second time, skip the 1st ending and play the 2nd ending.

## BLACKBERRY BLOSSOM

This traditional melody is a great workout across the five strings you've learned so far. These pieces are typically played fast, but take your time and focus on equal volume and steady rhythm.

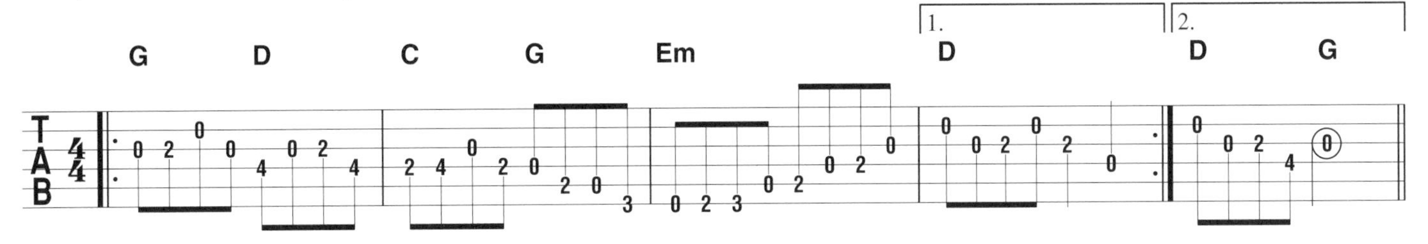

# THE HIGH E STRING

Here are the notes within the first five frets of the 1st string, called the E string.

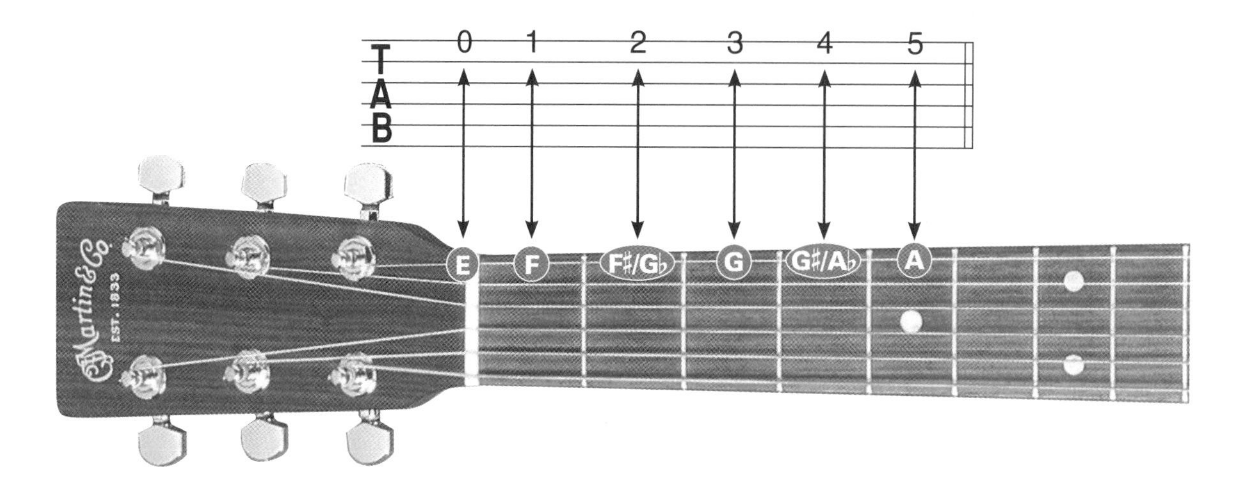


## IN MY LIFE

The opening riff of this song by the Beatles uses notes on the top two strings. Fret-hand fingerings are indicated below the tab staff.

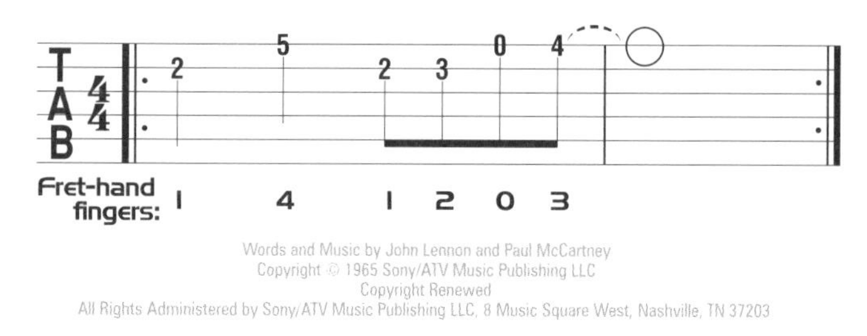




## TICKET TO RIDE

Here's another classic intro by the Beatles. Keep your 1st finger planted on the first note and let the strings ring throughout.

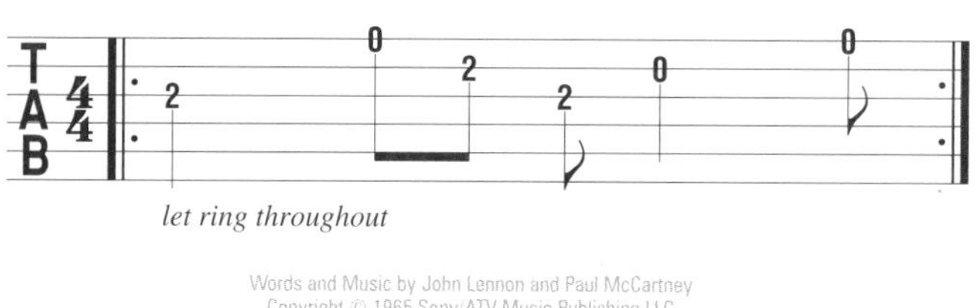




## WISH YOU WERE HERE

David Gilmour's acoustic guitar solo in the intro to this Pink Floyd classic features **slides**. As you pick the 5th string, quickly slide your index finger from the 1st to 2nd fret. In the next phrase, slide into the double stop from the 3rd to the 5th fret.

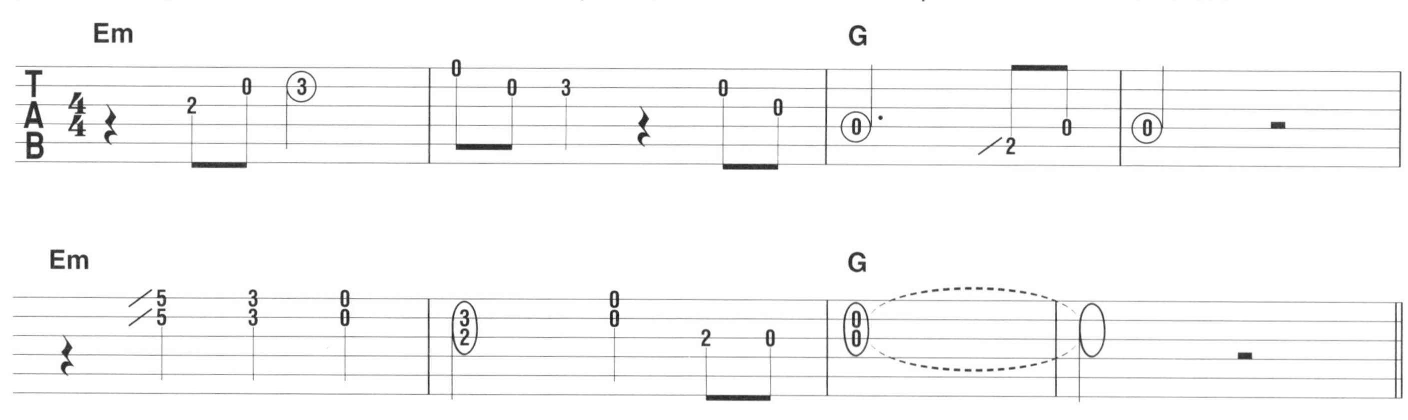

**Legato** techniques like hammer-ons, pull-offs, and slides, allow you to connect two or more consecutive notes with only a single pick attack, to create a smooth, flowing sound. These techniques are indicated with a curved line called a **slur** connecting the notes.

## HAMMER-ON

To play a **hammer-on**, pick the first note and then press down, or "hammer on" to, a higher note along the same string.

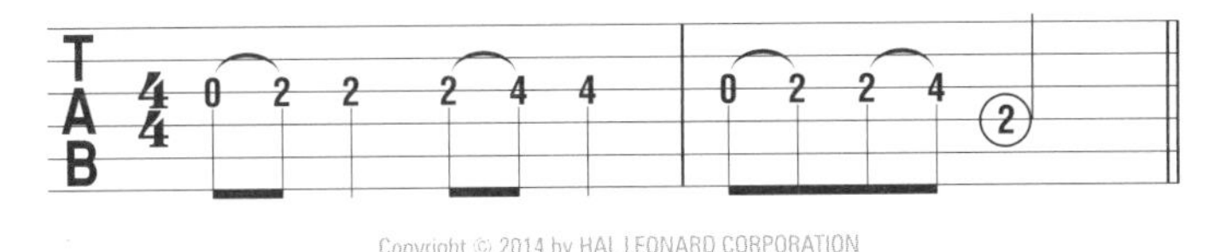




## PULL-OFF

A **pull-off** is just the opposite. Start with both fingers on their respective notes, pick the higher one, then tug or "pull" that finger off the string to sound the lower, already fretted note.

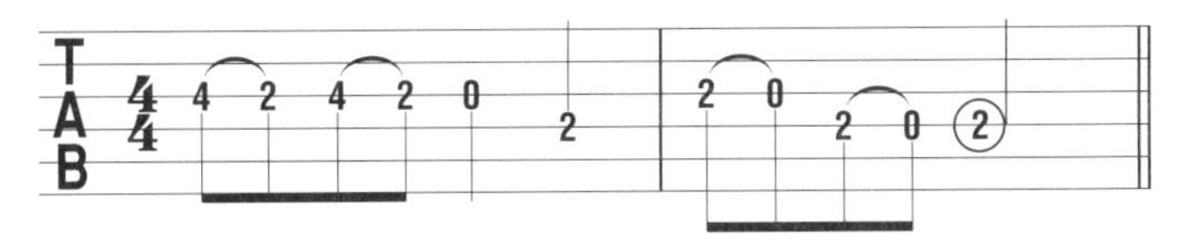

## LESTER'S LEAD

Guitarist Lester Flatt, of the legendary bluegrass duo Flatt & Scruggs, used the scalar pattern seen here over the G and C chords in measures 1 and 3, respectively, so often it's become known as the "Lester Flatt run."

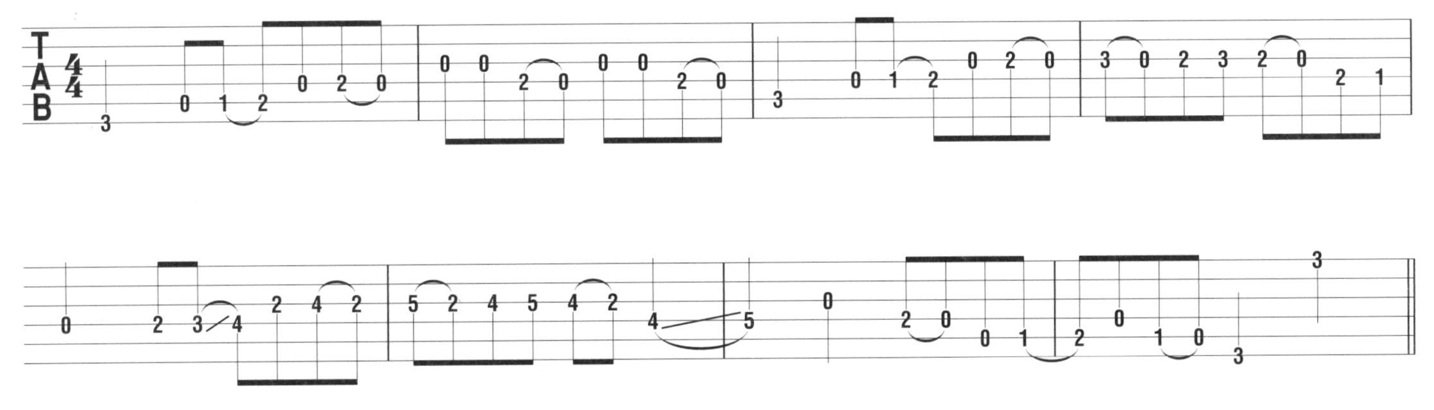




## WHISKEY BEFORE BREAKFAST

Guitarists typically use flatpicking when playing over bluegrass and Celtic tunes like this one, but these melodies also present great opportunities to work on hammer-ons and pull-offs.

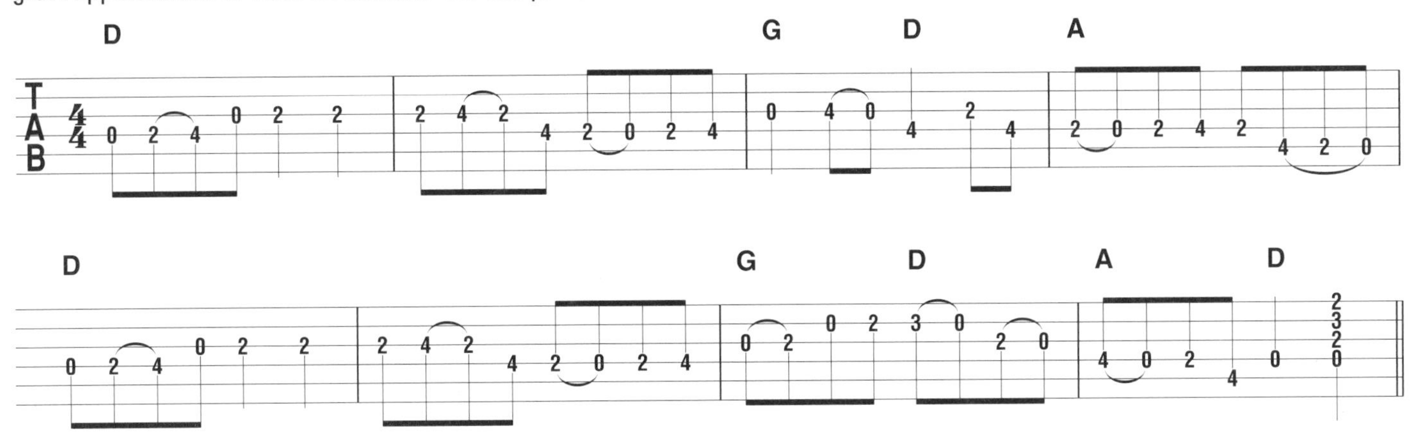


Traditional

# ARPEGGIOS

When a chord is played one note at a time, rather than strummed, it's called an **arpeggio**. You might also hear it called a "broken chord."

## BROKEN UP

Here's an example of an **ascending** arpeggio; that is, the notes are played from low to high.

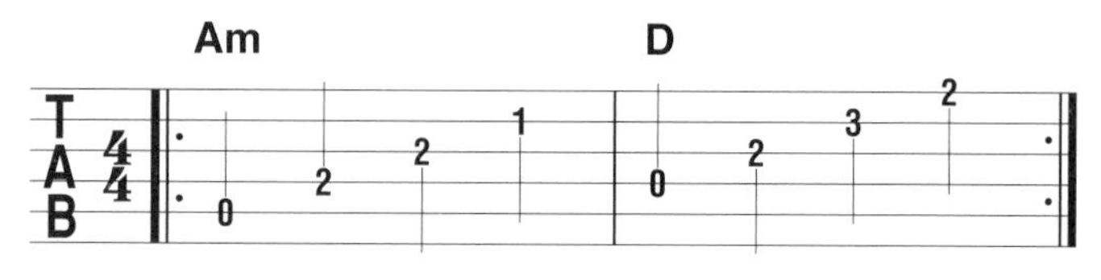




## BROKEN DOWN

Conversely, if you play the notes from high to low, it's called a **descending** arpeggio.

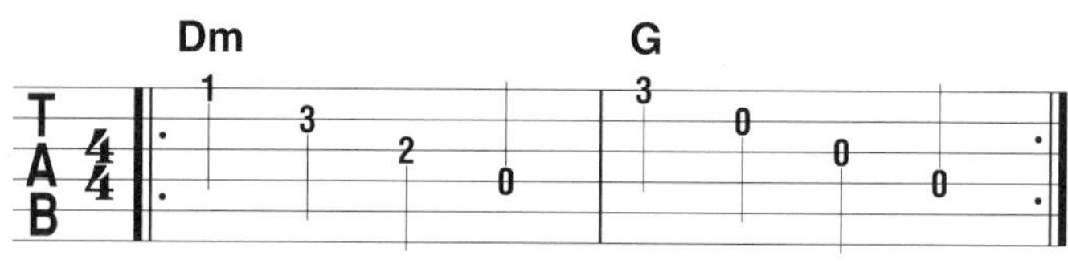




## CRIMSON AND CLOVER

In the breakdown of this Tommy James classic, the arpeggios are played both ascending and descending.

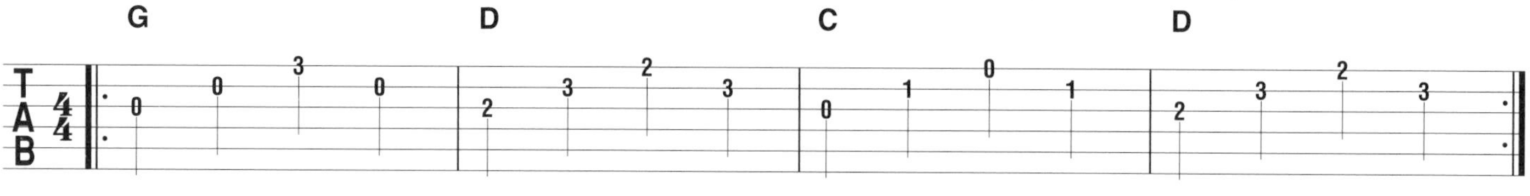




## LAST KISS

More often than not, you'll skip strings when playing arpeggios, as in this Pearl Jam ode to the doo-wop era.

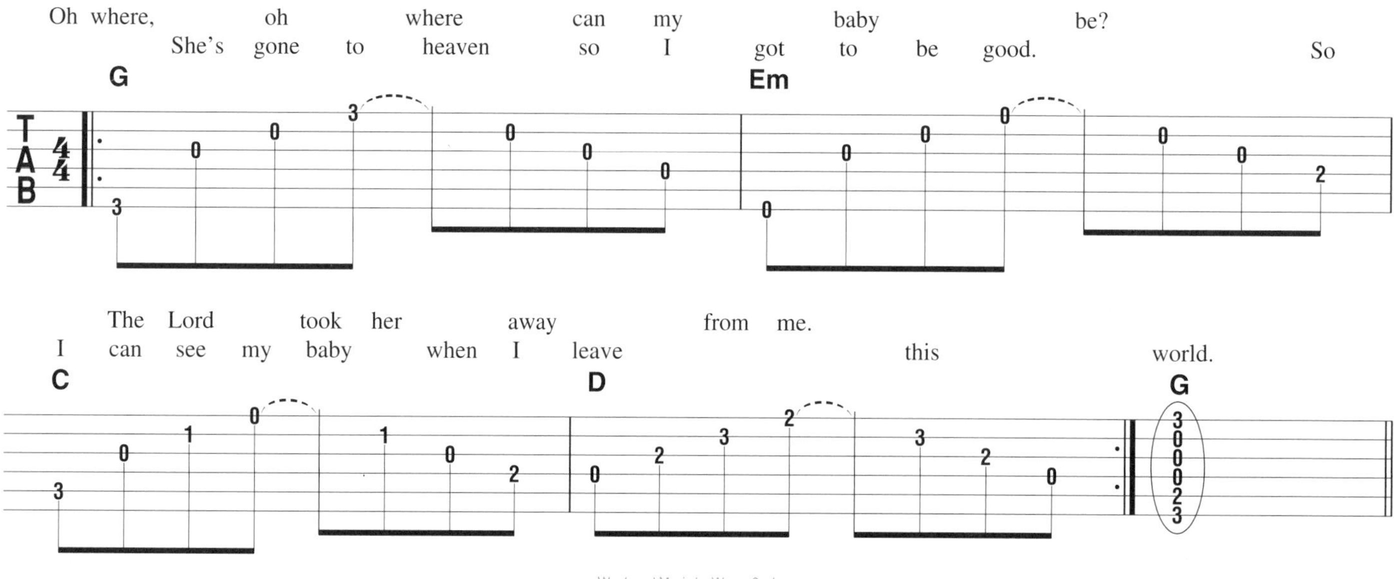




## MORE THAN A FEELING

Originally played on a 12-string, this Boston classic features a must-know arpeggio technique: the descending bass line. Tip: Keep your 3rd finger anchored on the 2nd string's 3rd fret throughout the riff.

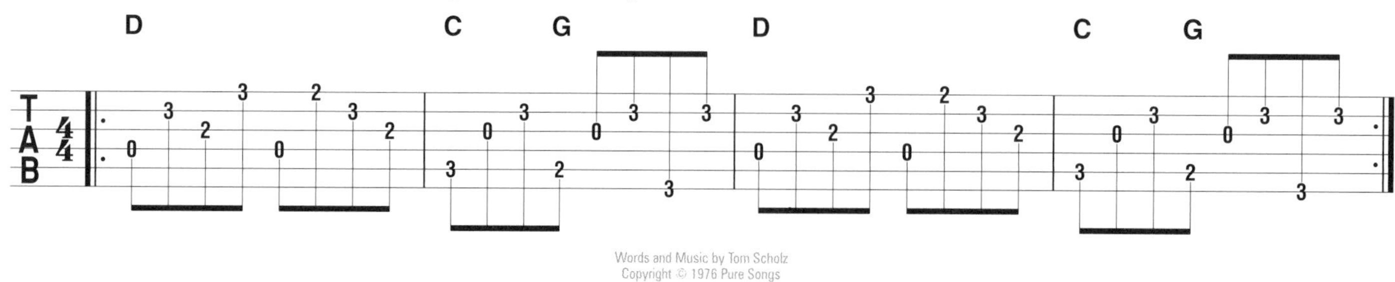

# WONDERFUL TONIGHT

Use a combination of arpeggios and strummed chords to play this beautiful Eric Clapton ballad.

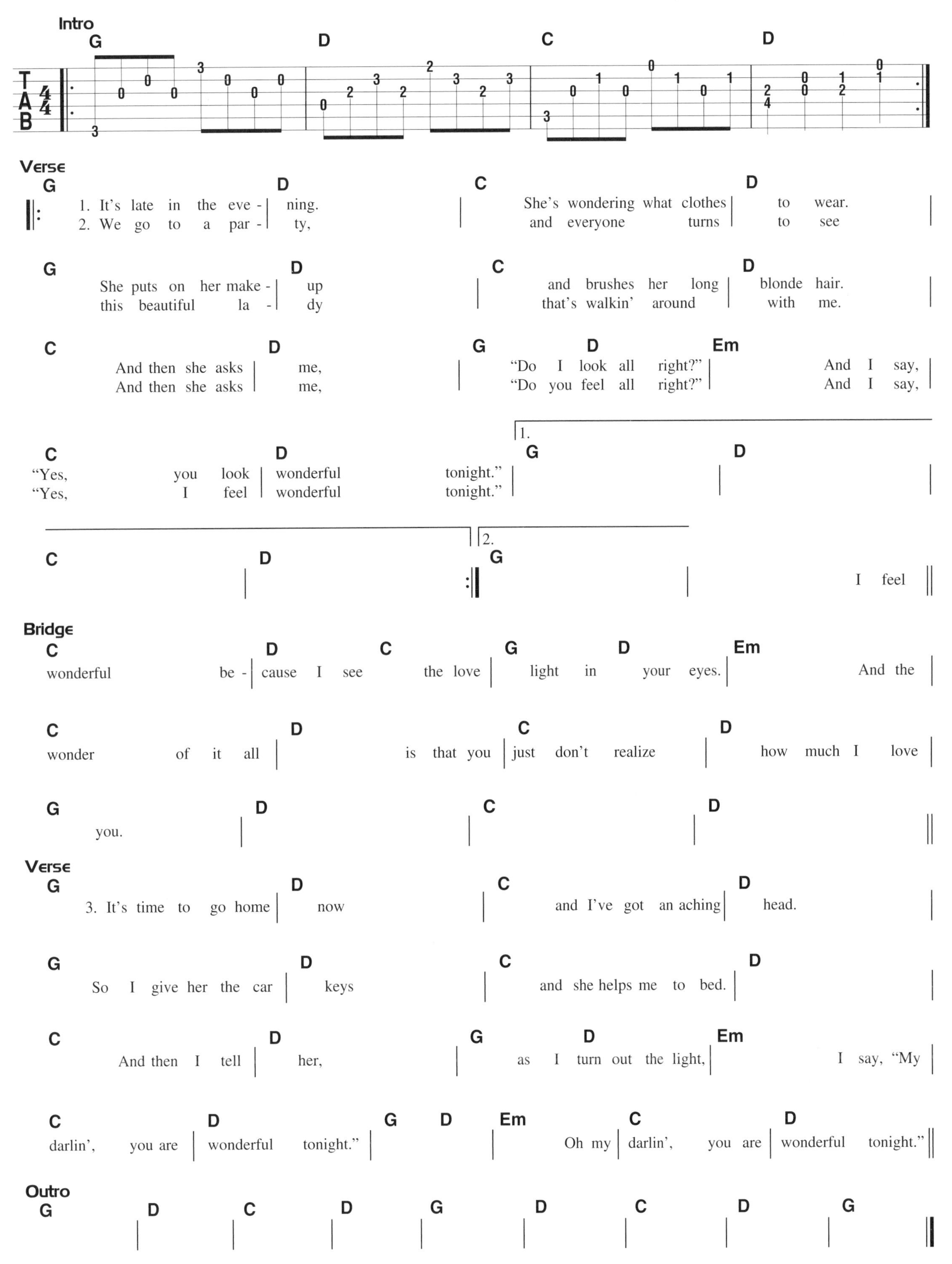

# PEACEFUL EASY FEELING

Here is the Eagles' classic strummer "Peaceful Easy Feeling" in chord-chart format. Use the audio as a strumming guide or improvise your own patterns.

**Intro**

4/4 ‖: D :‖ *play 4 times*

**Verse**

‖: D | G | D | G |
1. I like the way your sparklin' ear - rings lay
2. And I found out a long time ago
3. I get this feel - ing I may know you

| D | G | A | D |
against your skin so brown. And I wanna
what a woman can do to your soul. Ah, but she
as a lov - er and a friend. But this voice keeps

| G | D | G | D | G |
sleep with you in the desert tonight with a billion stars all around.
can't take you any - way you don't already know how to go.
whispering in my other ear, tells me I may never see you again.

**Chorus**

| A | 'Cause I got a / And I got a / 'Cause I get a ‖ G peaceful | easy feel - | D ing |

| G and I know you won't | let me down | Em | A 'cause I'm |

| D al - | Em ready stand - | G ing | 1., 2. A on the ground. | D |

| | | :‖ 3. A I'm | D al - | Em ready |

| G standing, | A yes, I'm | D al - | Em ready | G standing |

| A on the ground. | D | Em | G | A | D ‖